Insulin Resistance DIET COOKBOOK for Beginners

CATHERINE WADE

First Edition

Table of Contents

WEEK 4 133

BONUS RECIPES 165

Your Free Gift

As you embark on your Insulin Resistance Diet, it's essential to maintain a careful record of your dietary choices and blood sugar levels. Claim your complimentary Daily Food & Blood Sugar Tracker printables today to assist you in this important task.

To get instant access go to: https://cw.squarereads.com/insres

YOUR FREE PRINTABLES INCLUDE EVERYTHING YOU NEED:

- Daily Tracker

- Notes

You can organize these pages in a ring binder, and methodically document every aspect of your journey. This meticulous record-keeping will be invaluable as you work towards better health.

To start, I recommend printing out 28 Daily Tracker pages and 4 Notes pages to insert at the end of each week.

DAILY FOOD & BLOOD SUGAR TRACKER

CATHERINE WADE

Introduction

A few years ago, I went through a highly stressful situation. It was one of those experiences that never seemed to end. As a result, my health began to deteriorate. Apart from being put on tablets to manage my high blood pressure, I was also diagnosed with insulin resistance.

I was unfamiliar with the term insulin resistance, which prompted a visit to a nutritionist. The nutritionist not only clarified the concept but also provided guidance on foods to include and avoid to prevent further health complications.

Although I was provided with a lot of information, I was not given a meal plan to follow or recipes, which would have made it easier for me to adapt to a new way of eating. All in all, I found this completely overwhelming because, although I didn't feel vibrant and healthy, I felt normal.

Balancing the demands of each week consumed all my energy, making it challenging to prioritize my health. Many may not understand this struggle, but, unfortunately, my focus was solely on navigating the current stressful challenges rather than embracing a proactive approach to my well-being.

Many people don't experience noticeable symptoms, and I was one of them. Although I was not feeling particularly healthy, I also felt fine. I just wanted to get through the current situation I was experiencing, and then I would shift my focus to my health.

I don't recommend this approach.

Change is hard, and there will always be reasons why now is not the right time. If I had heeded the warnings back then, I probably wouldn't be suffering from to type 2 diabetes today and all the consequences of living with this avoidable disease.

If you're reading this book, you probably have good reason to make the recommended changes now.

This book contains an overview of insulin resistance, as well as weekly meal plans and shopping lists for the recipes, all provided to me by a registered dietician. I have taken the guesswork out to make this transition easy for you.

However, I recommend using this book in conjunction with a healthcare professional.

Delaying change may lead to irreversible consequences, and taking proactive steps toward a healthier lifestyle now is the best investment you can make in your long-term well-being.

Who Can Benefit From An Insulin Resistance Diet?

An insulin resistance diet holds immense value for those facing various health challenges. Anyone looking to prevent or reverse insulin resistance and associated health issues can proactively embrace it for long-term well-being.

Understanding that this dietary approach also extends its benefits to other conditions underscores its versatility and applicability. Individuals with various health issues can find valuable insights for enhancing their overall health and vitality. Although this chapter explores the diverse conditions and situations where adopting an insulin resistance diet can offer significant health benefits, it is always advisable to discuss this with a healthcare professional first to ensure it is the right diet for you.

Pre-Diabetic Individuals

Those diagnosed as pre-diabetic can leverage an insulin resistance diet to manage blood sugar levels effectively, preventing the progression to full-blown diabetes.

Type 2 Diabetes Management

Individuals with type 2 diabetes can find valuable support in an insulin resistance diet to regulate blood sugar, potentially reducing dependence on medication and managing the condition more effectively.

Metabolic Syndrome

Metabolic syndrome, marked by a group of conditions like elevated blood pressure, increased blood sugar, surplus body fat, and irregular cholesterol levels, can see beneficial effects with the adoption of dietary guidelines similar to those found in an insulin resistance diet.

Cardiovascular Health

The diet's emphasis on whole, nutrient-dense foods and reduced processed and refined items can contribute to cardiovascular health by managing blood pressure and cholesterol levels.

Weight Management

Those aiming for weight loss can also benefit from an insulin resistance diet, as it promotes a balanced intake of macronutrients, supports metabolism, and helps control hunger.

Polycystic Ovary Syndrome (PCOS)

Women with PCOS, often associated with insulin resistance, can find relief in managing symptoms through a diet that focuses on stabilizing blood sugar levels.

Gestational Diabetes

Pregnant women diagnosed with gestational diabetes can benefit from an insulin resistance diet to regulate blood sugar levels, supporting both maternal and fetal health.

Chronic Inflammation

Given its anti-inflammatory properties, certain conditions linked to chronic inflammation, such as arthritis and some autoimmune disorders, may improve with an insulin resistance diet.

Adopting an insulin resistance diet can be a proactive step toward overall health and wellness, even for individuals without specific health concerns. It promotes balanced nutrition, sustained energy levels, and a reduced risk of developing insulin-related issues in the future.

Benefits

Embarking on the insulin resistance diet isn't just about managing a specific health condition - it's a journey toward holistic well-being. The benefits extend beyond addressing insulin resistance, touching various facets of your health and daily life.

Improved Blood Sugar Control

At the core of the insulin resistance diet lies its ability to regulate blood sugar levels effectively. By choosing nutrient-dense foods and managing carbohydrate intake, individuals experience more stable blood sugar levels, reducing the risk of insulin resistance progression and related complications.

Enhanced Insulin Sensitivity

As the name suggests, the diet aims to improve insulin sensitivity. This means cells respond more efficiently to insulin signals, promoting better glucose absorption and utilization. Improved insulin sensitivity is a cornerstone in preventing and managing insulin resistance.

Sustainable Weight Management

Balanced meals, portion control, and nutrient-dense food choices contribute to effective weight management. Maintaining a healthy weight is integral to managing insulin resistance and reducing the risk of associated conditions like type 2 diabetes.

Cardiovascular Health Support

This dietary approach, designed to manage insulin resistance, aids in promoting cardiovascular well-being by targeting risk factors such as hypertension and irregular cholesterol levels. The focus on heart-healthy fats, fiber, and antioxidants contributes to overall cardiovascular well-being.

Increased Energy Levels

The diet provides a steady source of energy through well-balanced meals, helping prevent energy crashes and fatigue associated with fluctuating blood sugar levels. This sustained energy is crucial for daily activities and overall vitality.

Prevention and Management of Type 2 Diabetes

For individuals with prediabetes or at risk of type 2 diabetes, the insulin resistance diet offers a proactive approach. Addressing insulin resistance early significantly reduces the likelihood of progressing to full-blown diabetes.

Hormonal Balance for PCOS

The diet's impact extends to hormonal balance, making it particularly beneficial for individuals with Polycystic Ovary Syndrome (PCOS). Managing insulin resistance helps alleviate symptoms and supports reproductive and metabolic health.

Gut Health Improvement

Focusing on whole, unprocessed, fiber-rich foods promotes a healthy gut microbiome. A balanced gut contributes to better digestion, nutrient absorption, and overall digestive well-being.

Reduced Inflammation

Chronic inflammation is a precursor to various health issues. The anti-inflammatory properties of the diet, derived from whole, unprocessed foods rich in antioxidants, can help reduce inflammation, contributing to better overall health.

Enhanced Mental and Emotional Well-being

Stable blood sugar levels play a role in mood regulation. The insulin resistance diet's impact on preventing energy crashes can contribute to a more stable mood and improved mental focus.

Long-Term Chronic Disease Prevention

By embracing a diet rich in nutrients and maintaining a balanced nutritional profile, individuals adhering to the principles of the insulin resistance diet could potentially lower their susceptibility to chronic ailments such as cardiovascular diseases, specific types of cancer, and neurodegenerative disorders.

The insulin resistance diet represents a holistic lifestyle strategy that tackles individual health issues while fostering general well-being and longevity. Its transformative advantages encompass various aspects of overall health, rendering it a worthwhile commitment to long-term health and vitality.

Understanding Insulin Resistance

In the complex interplay of hormones governing our body's functions, insulin assumes a central role. Unraveling the role of insulin in our physiology is crucial to comprehending the concept of insulin resistance.

The Role of Insulin

Insulin, generated by the pancreas, is a hormone that plays a key role in managing blood sugar levels. Its primary function is facilitating glucose absorption into cells, providing them with the energy they need for proper functioning. In simpler terms, insulin is the key that unlocks cells, allowing glucose to enter.

The Mechanism of Insulin Resistance

Insulin resistance arises when the body's cells exhibit reduced sensitivity to insulin signals. Think of it as the cells changing their locks, making it challenging for insulin to do its job effectively. Consequently, glucose accumulates in the bloodstream, leading to elevated blood sugar levels.

Causes of Insulin Resistance

Understanding the factors contributing to insulin resistance is essential for proactive management. Genetics, lifestyle decisions, and environmental influences each contribute to this phenomenon. Sedentary behavior, inadequate dietary patterns, and obesity are frequently implicated, creating favorable conditions for the onset of insulin resistance.

Health Implications

Insulin resistance isn't merely a glitch in the system; it's a precursor to various health issues. It significantly increases the risk of developing type 2 diabetes, cardiovascular diseases, and metabolic syndrome. Recognizing the potential consequences underscores the urgency of addressing insulin resistance early on.

Signs and Symptoms

Identifying insulin resistance early can be challenging as it often manifests subtly. Fatigue, weight gain, increased thirst, and frequent urination are common indicators. Being attuned to these signs allows for timely intervention, preventing the progression of insulin resistance to more severe health conditions.

Importance of Detection and Intervention

Knowledge is power, and early detection of insulin resistance empowers individuals to take charge of their health. This chapter emphasizes the significance of proactive intervention, setting the stage for the subsequent chapters, which explore effective strategies, lifestyle changes, and a tailored diet plan to manage insulin resistance and promote overall well-being.

Why You Don't Want To Develop Type 2 Diabetes

The chronic medical condition known as type 2 diabetes arises when the body either produces insufficient insulin or develops resistance to its effects, leading to difficulty in maintaining normal blood sugar levels.

It's essential to avoid developing type 2 diabetes for several reasons:

Health Complications

If poorly managed or left untreated, type 2 diabetes can result in serious health complications. These may include heart disease, stroke, kidney problems, nerve damage, and vision issues.

Quality of Life

Living with uncontrolled diabetes can significantly impact your daily life. It may lead to fatigue, frequent urination, excessive thirst, and other symptoms that affect your overall well-being and quality of life.

Increased Risk of Other Conditions

Individuals with type 2 diabetes are increasingly at risk of developing other significant health issues, such as high blood pressure and high cholesterol. These conditions, when combined, elevate the risk of cardiovascular diseases.

Long-Term Health Care Costs

Managing diabetes and its associated complications can result in significant healthcare expenses. Regular medical check-ups, medications, and potential hospitalizations can be financially burdensome.

Lifestyle Changes

Developing type 2 diabetes often necessitates significant lifestyle changes, including modifications to your diet, exercise routine, and overall daily habits. Prevention is preferable to having to make substantial adjustments later in life.

Preventable with Healthy Lifestyle Choices

Type 2 diabetes, in many cases, is preventable through lifestyle choices. Adhering to a healthy weight, regular physical activity, and a well-balanced diet can markedly diminish the likelihood of developing this condition.

Impact on Mental Health

The constant management of diabetes, coupled with the potential for complications, can have an impact on mental health. The strain of coping with a chronic condition and the fear of potential complications can result in feelings of anxiety and depression.

Long-Term Consequences

Type 2 diabetes is a progressive condition. Over time, uncontrolled diabetes can affect various organs and systems in the body, leading to irreversible damage. Preventing its onset is crucial for long-term health.

Embracing a healthy lifestyle, which encompasses a balanced diet, consistent exercise, and the maintenance of a healthy weight, is crucial. This approach can notably mitigate the risk of developing type 2 diabetes. Additionally, scheduling regular check-ups with healthcare providers can aid in early detection and effective management if any risk factors are identified.

What To Avoid

If you're following an insulin resistance diet, avoiding or limiting certain foods that can spike blood sugar levels and contribute to insulin resistance is beneficial. Here are some foods you may want to be cautious about:

Highly Processed Foods

Foods with added sugars, refined grains, and unhealthy fats can contribute to insulin resistance. Examples include sugary snacks, pastries, and many packaged convenience foods.

Sugary Beverages

Drinks with added sugars, such as sodas, certain fruit juices, and sweetened teas, can cause blood sugar to spike and should be limited or avoided.

Simple Carbohydrates

Foods made with white flour, white rice, and other refined grains can quickly raise blood sugar levels. Opt for whole grains instead.

Sweets and Desserts

Cakes, cookies, candies, and similar sugary treats should be enjoyed sparingly, considering their elevated sugar levels.

Highly Processed Meats

Processed meats like sausages, hot dogs, and certain processed deli meats often contain additives and preservatives that may contribute to insulin resistance. Choose lean, unprocessed protein sources instead.

Fried Foods

Fried foods, especially those cooked in unhealthy oils, can harm insulin sensitivity. Opt for cooking methods like baking, grilling, or steaming instead.

Fruit Juices

While whole fruits are generally healthy, fruit juices can concentrate the sugars without the fiber found in whole fruits. It's better to eat whole fruits in moderation.

Sweetened Yogurts

Flavored yogurts often contain added sugars. For sweetness, choose plain, unsweetened yogurt and add fresh that are used in the meal plans.

Alcohol

Overindulging in alcohol can disrupt blood sugar levels and exacerbate insulin resistance. If you opt to consume alcohol, do so in moderation.

Highly Sweetened Condiments

Some condiments, like ketchup and barbecue sauce, can contain a lot of added sugars. Opt for alternatives with little to no added sugars.

Keep in mind that individual reactions to foods vary, so it's important to monitor how your body responds. Prioritize a balanced diet rich in whole, nutrient-dense foods like vegetables, lean proteins, healthy fats, and complex carbohydrates. If you have dietary needs, seek advice from a healthcare provider or registered dietitian for tailored recommendations.

Cultivating The Right Mindset Before Starting The Insulin Resistance Diet

Embarking on the insulin resistance diet is not just a shift in eating habits; it's a journey that requires the right mindset for sustainable success and the importance of cultivating a positive and proactive mental attitude before starting the diet.

Understanding Your Why

Before exploring dietary modifications, consider why you're choosing the insulin resistance diet. Whether your motivations are to manage insulin resistance, prevent diabetes, or enhance overall well-being, a clear understanding of your motivations will anchor your commitment.

Understanding the Power of Mindset

The first step is to recognize that your mindset plays a pivotal role in achieving health goals. Your attitude, beliefs, and outlook influence your ability to make lasting changes in your lifestyle. By understanding the power of mindset, you set the stage for a successful journey toward managing insulin resistance.

Acknowledging Challenges

Change is seldom easy, and acknowledging potential challenges is crucial. Whether it's adjusting to new dietary preferences or overcoming emotional eating habits, recognizing challenges empowers you to develop strategies to overcome them, fostering resilience in the face of adversity.

Shifting Focus to Long-Term Health

Rather than fixating on short-term goals or immediate results, shift your focus to long-term health. The insulin resistance diet is not a quick fix but a sustainable approach to well-being. Consider the lasting benefits you're investing in.

Setting Realistic Expectations

Establishing realistic expectations is essential for long-term success. Recognize that embracing a new dietary approach can be gradual, and results may take time.

Setting achievable short-term goals and celebrating small victories can keep you motivated.

Seeking Support

Building a support system is integral to success. Share your goals with friends, family, or a healthcare professional who can provide encouragement, advice, and understanding.

Practicing Mindful Eating

Mindful eating involves:
- Being attuned to your body's signals of hunger and fullness.
- Savoring each bite.
- Being present during meals.

By integrating mindfulness into your dietary habits, you cultivate a more wholesome connection with food and enrich your overall eating experience.

Celebrating Progress

Celebrate your achievements along the way. Whether it's reaching a weight loss milestone, consistently adhering to the diet, or noticing improvements in energy levels, acknowledging and celebrating your progress reinforces positive behaviors and boosts motivation.

Staying Open-Minded

Maintain an open mind as you explore new foods and eating patterns. Be willing to experiment with recipes, try different approaches, and discover what works best for you. An open-minded approach fosters adaptability and allows for a more enjoyable dietary experience.

Visualizing Success

Envision the positive outcomes of managing insulin resistance and adopting a healthier lifestyle. Visualizing success helps reinforce your commitment and serves as a powerful motivator. Create mental images of a healthier, more vibrant you to inspire and guide your journey.

Cultivating the right mindset before starting the insulin resistance diet is foundational to success. By adopting a positive and proactive mental attitude, you lay the groundwork for lasting lifestyle changes that contribute to improved overall well-being.

Meal Plans, Shopping Lists And Recipes

This cookbook follows a **meal plan structure***, where all recipes are tailored to fit the plan's requirements. As a result, you'll find some basic recipes like baked potatoes, brown rice, and nuts included, even though they may seem unnecessary. These recipes ensure that every component used in the meal plan has a dedicated recipe page, complete with* **nutritional information and quantities.**

Please note the meal plans are general meal plans for recipes specifically for control of insulin resistance. They don't consider personal health issues, conditions, goals, other food intolerances, or allergies.

The 28-Day Meal Plan is divided into three, four weekly sections.

1. 7-Days Meal Plan
2. Shopping List
3. Recipes

Each week, there are recipes for breakfast, lunch, dinner, and snacks. The snacks can be eaten anytime. The food for each day has been nutritionally balanced, and this information is displayed at the end of each recipe. Each week has been color coded for easy reference.

We all have days where we sometimes require more food, and with this in mind, you can enjoy something extra from the **Bonus Recipes** chapter.

When you first start your meal plan, there will be ingredients on your shopping list that you may not already have in your pantry. You will need to purchase these, however, as often only a little is used, many won't have to be repurchased.

If any food item is unfamiliar, please refer to the **Food Translations** page at the back of the book. Often, common foods are known by different names around the world.

Cooking Conversions are at the back of the book to guide you if needed.

WEEK 1

All weeks follow the same format with a meal plan for the week and a shopping list for the recipe ingredients.

Before you start cooking, assemble all the ingredients, and prep them according to the ingredients list.

Every recipe states the total number of servings and the total prep time so that you know how many servings the recipe creates, and how long it will take you to make it.

Most recipes are for one serving. For more servings, increase the ingredients and adjust the recipe accordingly. If a recipe is for two servings, then halve the ingredients if only cooking for one.

7-Days Meal Plan

MONDAY

BREAKFAST
Feta Scrambled Eggs & Raspberries, Almonds

LUNCH
Butternut Squash, Sage & Kale Frittata, Orange

DINNER
Baked Cod with Chickpeas & Tomatoes, Apple

SNACKS
Grilled Apricots with Yogurt & Pistachios

TUESDAY

BREAKFAST
Greek Yogurt with Orange, Blueberries & Pumpkin Seeds

LUNCH
Kale & Purple Cabbage Beef Hash, Kiwi

DINNER
Chicken & Asparagus Pesto Pasta, Blueberries

SNACKS
Lemon Dill Yogurt Dip with Carrots & Celery

WEDNESDAY

BREAKFAST
One Pan Cauliflower, Mushroom & Egg, Mango Smoothie

LUNCH
Grilled Chicken with Cucumber Salad, Grapes

DINNER
Baked Salmon with Broccoli & Quinoa, Fresh Strawberries

SNACKS
Snap Peas & Hummus

THURSDAY

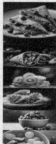

BREAKFAST
Coconut Blueberry Crepes

LUNCH
Turkey, Avocado & Black Bean Wrap, Kiwi

DINNER
Beef & Chickpea Lettuce Wraps, Blueberries

SNACKS
Grapes & Almonds

FRIDAY

BREAKFAST
Jammy Eggs on Yogurt Toast

LUNCH
Olive, Mushroom & Feta Frittata, Pear

DINNER
One Pan Tuna Steak & Bell Peppers, Grapes

SNACKS
Pistachio Trail Mix

SATURDAY

BREAKFAST
Avocado Toast with Hard Boiled Eggs & Strawberries

LUNCH
Tuna Stuffed Pepper, Easy Home Salad

DINNER
Salmon, Collard Greens & Cauliflower, Kiwi

SNACKS
Coconut Yogurt, Strawberries & Blackberries

SUNDAY

BREAKFAST
Raspberry Pecan Warm Chia Pudding

LUNCH
Poached Salmon, Artichokes & Sweet Potato, Orange

DINNER
Lemon & Asparagus Chicken Skillet, Apple

SNACKS
Yogurt & Fresh Apricots

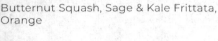
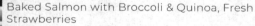

Shopping List

FRUITS
2 Apples
3 Apricots
1 Avocado
1 Banana
1 cup Blackberries
2 ⅓ cups Blueberries
3 cups Grapes
6 Kiwi
⅔ Lemon
1 tbsp Lemon Juice
2 ½ Navel Oranges
1 Pear
1 cup Raspberries
2 ¼ cups Strawberries

SEEDS, NUTS & SPICES
⅔ cup Almonds
2 ⅔ tbsps Cashews
3 tbsps Chia Seeds
1 ¹⁄₁₆ tsp Cumin
⅛ tsp Dried Rosemary
⅛ tsp Dried Thyme
⅛ tsp Garlic Powder
2 ⅔ tbsps Goji Berries
1 tsp Ground Flax Seeds
2 tbsps Pecans
2 ⅔ tbsps Pistachios
1 ½ tbsps Walnuts
Sea Salt & Black Pepper

FROZEN
2 tbsps Frozen Blueberries
½ cup Frozen Cauliflower

VEGETABLES
1 ½ cups Asparagus
¼ cup Basil Leaves
⅛ head Boston Lettuce
1 cup Broccoli

1 ¾ cups Butternut Squash
1 Carrot
⅓ head Cauliflower
1 stalk Celery
1 cup Cherry Tomatoes
1 ½ cups Collard Greens
2 ¾ cups Cremini Mushrooms
¾ Cucumber
3 ¾ tbsps Fresh Dill
¾ tsp Fresh Sage
3 Garlic
⅛ head Green Lettuce
2 stalks Green Onion
1 ½ cups Kale Leaves
½ cup Mixed Greens
½ Orange Bell Pepper
1 ½ tbsps Parsley
1 cup Purple Cabbage
1 ½ Red Bell Peppers
½ cup Shallot
1 cup Snap Peas
½ Sweet Potato
½ Tomato
⅛ Yellow Onion

PANTRY STAPLES
⅓ cup Black Beans
70 grams Chickpea Pasta
1 cup Chickpeas
½ cup Diced Tomatoes
¼ cup Quinoa
1 can Tuna
1 cup Vegetable Broth (low sodium)
½ cup Artichoke Hearts
1 tbsp Pitted Kalamata Olives

BAKING
2 tbsps Almond Butter

BREAD, FISH, MEAT & CHEESE
188 grams Chicken Breast
113 grams Chicken Thighs
1 Cod Fillet
2 tbsps Cream Cheese (regular)
233 grams Lean Ground Beef
2 ¼ Parmigiano Reggiano
480 grams Salmon Fillets
140 grams Tuna Steak
113 grams Turkey Breast (cooked)
3 slices Whole Grain Bread
1 Whole Wheat Tortilla

CONDIMENTS & OILS
1 ½ tsps Apple Cider Vinegar
2 tsps Coconut Oil
⅓ cup Extra Virgin Olive Oil
1 ⅓ tbsps Pesto
1 ½ Red Wine Vinegar
1 tsp Whole Grain Mustard

FRIDGE
1 tsp Butter
13 Eggs
½ cup Hummus
2 cups Plain Greek Yogurt
1 cup Unsweetened Almond Milk
1 ½ cups Unsweetened Coconut Yogurt

Breakfasts

Feta Scrambled Eggs & Raspberries

 10 Minutes

 1 Serving

INGREDIENTS

- ¼ cup Feta Cheese (crumbled)
- Sea Salt & Black Pepper (to taste)
- 3 Eggs (whisked)
- 1 tsp Butter
- ½ cup Raspberries

INSTRUCTIONS

1. Add the feta, salt, and pepper to the whisked eggs. Stir until well combined.
2. Melt the butter in a pan over a medium heat. Add the egg mix and gently scramble until cooked to your desired doneness.
3. Add the cooked eggs and raspberries to a plate.

NUTRITION - AMOUNT PER SERVING

Calories	380	Sugar	3g
Fat	27g	Protein	25g
Carbs	10g	Cholesterol	602mg
Fiber	4g	Sodium	641mg

Almonds

 2 Minutes

 1 Serving

INGREDIENTS

- ¼ cup Almonds (raw)

INSTRUCTIONS

1. Place the almonds in a bowl and enjoy!

NUTRITION - AMOUNT PER SERVING

Calories	207	Sugar	2g
Fat	18g	Protein	8g
Carbs	8g	Cholesterol	0mg
Fiber	4g	Sodium	0mg

Greek Yogurt with Orange, Blueberries & Pumpkin Seeds

 5 Minutes

 1 Serving

INGREDIENTS

- 1 cup Plain Greek Yogurt
- ½ Navel Orange (chopped)
- ⅓ cup Blueberries
- 2 tbsps Pumpkin Seeds

INSTRUCTIONS

1. Add all the ingredients to a bowl and enjoy!

NUTRITION - AMOUNT PER SERVING

Calories	333	Sugar	17g
Fat	13g	Protein	28g
Carbs	30g	Cholesterol	34mg
Fiber	4g	Sodium	142mg

One Pan Cauliflower, Mushroom & Egg

 20 Minutes

 1 Serving

INGREDIENTS

- ½ tsp Extra Virgin Olive Oil
- ⅛ head Cauliflower (small, chopped into florets)
- 2 Cremini Mushrooms (sliced)
- 2 Eggs
- 1 ½ tsps Fresh Dill
- Sea Salt & Black Pepper (to taste)

INSTRUCTIONS

1. In a non-stick pan, warm the olive oil over medium heat.
2. Add the cauliflower and cook for 7 to 8 minutes, stirring often to cook evenly until becoming tender.
3. Next, add mushrooms to the pan and cook for a few minutes until browned.
4. Whisk together the eggs, dill, salt, and pepper in a bowl. Pour into the pan and turn the heat down to low. Cook for about 6 to 7 minutes or until the egg has set.
5. Plate and enjoy!

NUTRITION - AMOUNT PER SERVING

Calories	189	Sugar	3g
Fat	12g	Protein	15g
Carbs	6g	Cholesterol	372mg
Fiber	2g	Sodium	166mg

Mango Smoothie

 5 Minutes

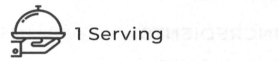 1 Serving

INGREDIENTS

- ½ cup Frozen Mango
- ½ cup Frozen Cauliflower
- 1 Banana (medium)
- 1 ½ cups Water
- 1 ½ tsps Apple Cider Vinegar

INSTRUCTIONS

1. Place all ingredients in a blender and blend until smooth. Pour into a glass and enjoy!

NUTRITION - AMOUNT PER SERVING

Calories	173	Sugar	27g
Fat	1g	Protein	3g
Carbs	43g	Cholesterol	0mg
Fiber	7g	Sodium	26mg

Coconut Blueberry Crepes

 15 Minutes

 1 Serving

INGREDIENTS

- 2 tbsps Unsweetened Almond Milk
- 2 tbsps Frozen Blueberries
- 1 Egg (large)
- 2 tbsps Coconut Flour
- 1/16 tsp Sea Salt
- 2 tsps Coconut Oil (divided)

INSTRUCTIONS

1. Add the milk, blueberries, egg, coconut flour, and salt to a blender. Blend all ingredients until smooth.
2. Over a medium heat, warm a little coconut oil in a non-stick pan. Pour ¼ cup of the batter and gently swirl to form a thin layer. Cook each side of the crepe for about 30 seconds to 1 minute. Repeat with the remaining batter and oil.
3. Plate and enjoy!

NUTRITION - AMOUNT PER SERVING

Calories	225	Sugar	3g
Fat	16g	Protein	8g
Carbs	11g	Cholesterol	186mg
Fiber	6g	Sodium	269mg

Jammy Eggs on Yogurt Toast

 10 Minutes

 1 Serving

INGREDIENTS

- 1 Egg
- ¼ cup Plain Greek Yogurt
- 1 tsp Fresh Dill (finely chopped)
- Sea Salt & Black Pepper (to taste)
- 1 slice Whole Grain Bread (toasted)
- ½ tsp Extra Virgin Olive Oil

INSTRUCTIONS

1. Add an egg to a small pot of boiling water and reduce the heat slightly. Cook for 6 minutes for a soft-boiled egg. Once the egg is done, add to a bowl of ice water and set aside.
2. In a small bowl mix together the yogurt and dill. Season with salt and pepper.
3. Spread the yogurt on the bread. Peel the egg, slice it in half, and place it on the yogurt. Splash the egg with olive oil and season with salt and pepper.

NUTRITION - AMOUNT PER SERVING

Calories	246	Sugar	4g
Fat	10g	Protein	17g
Carbs	21g	Cholesterol	194mg
Fiber	3g	Sodium	264mg

Avocado Toast with Hard Boiled Eggs & Strawberries

 15 Minutes

 1 Serving

INGREDIENTS

- 2 Eggs
- 2 slices Whole Grain Bread (toasted)
- ½ Avocado (sliced or mashed)
- 1 cup Strawberries

INSTRUCTIONS

1. Place the eggs in a saucepan and cover with water. Bring to a boil over high heat. Turn down the heat and simmer for about 6 to 10 minutes. Peel and slice the eggs when cool enough to handle.
2. Top the whole grain toast with the avocado and eggs. Serve alongside the strawberries.

NUTRITION - AMOUNT PER SERVING

Calories	569	Sugar	13g
Fat	28g	Protein	27g
Carbs	56g	Cholesterol	372mg
Fiber	16g	Sodium	465mg

Raspberry Pecan Warm Chia Pudding

 10 Minutes

 1 Serving

INGREDIENTS

- 3 tbsps Chia Seeds
- ¾ cup Unsweetened Almond Milk
- ½ cup Raspberries
- 2 tbsps Pecans
- 2 tbsps Almond Butter

INSTRUCTIONS

1. Over a medium-low heat, whisk the almond milk and chia seeds in a small pot. Continue until heated through and the mixture has thickened, about 5 minutes.
2. Remove from heat and add the mix to a bowl. Top with raspberries, pecans, and a dollop of almond butter.

NUTRITION - AMOUNT PER SERVING

Calories	505	Sugar	5g
Fat	40g	Protein	15g
Carbs	31g	Cholesterol	0mg
Fiber	21g	Sodium	128mg

Butternut Squash, Sage & Kale Frittata

 5 Minutes

 1 Serving

INGREDIENTS

- ½ tsp Extra Virgin Olive Oil
- ¾ cup Butternut Squash (seeds removed, cubed)
- ½ cup Kale Leaves (chopped)
- ½ Garlic (clove, minced)
- ¾ tsp Fresh Sage (chopped)
- Sea Salt & Black Pepper (to taste)
- 2 Eggs (whisked)

INSTRUCTIONS

1. Preheat oven to 400°F (205°C).
2. In an oven-safe pan, heat the oil over a medium heat. Add the butternut squash and sauté for about 5 minutes.
3. Add the kale, garlic, sage, salt, and pepper. Sauté for another minute before adding the whisked eggs to the pan.
4. Place the pan carefully in the preheated oven and bake until cooked, about 12 to 15 minutes.

NUTRITION - AMOUNT PER SERVING

Calories	218	Sugar	14g
Fat	3g	Protein	372mg
Carbs	12g	Cholesterol	3g
Fiber	14g	Sodium	152mg

Orange

 2 Minutes

 1 Serving

INGREDIENTS

- 1 Navel Orange

INSTRUCTIONS

1. Slice into wedges or peel and section.

NUTRITION - AMOUNT PER SERVING

Calories	69	Sugar	12g
Fat	0g	Protein	1g
Carbs	18g	Cholesterol	0mg
Fiber	3g	Sodium	1mg

Lunches

Kale & Purple Cabbage Beef Hash

 25 Minutes

 1 Serving

INGREDIENTS

- 1 ½ tsps Extra Virgin Olive Oil
- 113 grams Lean Ground Beef
- ¼ tsp Sea Salt (divided)
- ⅛ tsp Dried Rosemary
- ⅛ tsp Dried Thyme
- 1 cup Kale Leaves (finely chopped)
- 1 cup Purple Cabbage (finely chopped)

INSTRUCTIONS

1. In a large skillet, warm the oil over a medium heat.
2. Add the ground beef. Use a spatula to break it up as it cooks.
3. Season with rosemary, thyme, and half of the salt. Cook for 8 to 10 minutes or until cooked through.
4. Mix in the kale, cabbage, and remaining salt. Cook for 4 to 5 minutes or until the vegetables have softened. Serve in a bowl.

NUTRITION - AMOUNT PER SERVING

Calories	383	Sugar	18g
Fat	4g	Protein	81mg
Carbs	30g	Cholesterol	3g
Fiber	21g	Sodium	700mg

Kiwi

 5 Minutes

 1 Serving

INGREDIENTS

- 2 Kiwis

INSTRUCTIONS

1. Peel and slice.

NUTRITION - AMOUNT PER SERVING

Calories	84	Sugar	12g
Fat	1g	Protein	2g
Carbs	20g	Cholesterol	0g
Fiber	4g	Sodium	4mg

Grilled Chicken with Cucumber Salad

 25 Minutes    1 Serving

INGREDIENTS

- 113 grams Chicken Thighs (boneless, skinless)
- Sea Salt & Black Pepper (to taste)
- 1 tbsp Extra Virgin Olive Oil
- 1 ½ tsps Lemon Juice
- ½ cup Cherry Tomatoes (halved)
- ½ Cucumber (medium, diced)
- 2 tbsps Fresh Dill (chopped)

INSTRUCTIONS

1. Preheat a grill pan or grill over a medium heat.
2. Season the chicken with salt and pepper. Place on the preheated grill and cook for about 8 to 10 minutes per side, or until cooked through and charred. Remove from the grill and let rest for 2 minutes.
3. Meanwhile, combine the oil, lemon juice, tomatoes, cucumber, and dill in a bowl. Season to taste and set aside.
4. Serve the grilled chicken alongside the cucumber salad.

NUTRITION - AMOUNT PER SERVING

Calories	294	Sugar	5g
Fat	19g	Protein	24g
Carbs	9g	Cholesterol	106mg
Fiber	2g	Sodium	115mg

Grapes

 2 Minutes

 1 Serving

INGREDIENTS

- 1 cup Grapes

INSTRUCTIONS

1. Wash grapes, place in a bowl and enjoy!

NUTRITION - AMOUNT PER SERVING

Calories	62	Sugar	15g
Fat	0g	Protein	1g
Carbs	16g	Cholesterol	0mg
Fiber	1g	Sodium	2mg

Turkey, Avocado & Black Bean Wrap

 10 Minutes

 1 Serving

INGREDIENTS

- 1 Whole Wheat Tortilla (large)
- 2 tbsps Hummus
- ½ cup Mixed Greens
- 113 grams Cooked Turkey Breast, (shredded/sliced)
- ⅓ cup Black Beans (cooked)
- ½ Avocado (medium, sliced)
- Sea Salt & Black Pepper (to taste)

INSTRUCTIONS

1. Place the tortilla on a flat surface. Spread the hummus onto half and add the greens, turkey, beans, and avocado. Season with salt and pepper.
2. Roll up tightly into a wrap to enjoy!

NUTRITION - AMOUNT PER SERVING

Calories	594	Sugar	2g
Fat	27g	Protein	47g
Carbs	46g	Cholesterol	79mg
Fiber	18g	Sodium	529mg

REFER TO KIWI RECIPE PAGE 34 FOR QUANTITY AND NUTRITIONAL INFORMATION

Olive, Mushroom & Feta Frittata

 30 Minutes

 1 Serving

INGREDIENTS

- 2 tsps Extra Virgin Olive Oil
- 1/16 tsp Sea Salt
- 1 tbsp Pitted Kalamata Olives (sliced)
- ¾ Cremini Mushrooms (sliced)
- 2 Eggs (whisked)
- 1 tbsp Feta Cheese (crumbled)
- 1 ½ tsps Basil Leaves

INSTRUCTIONS

1. Preheat oven to 350°F (175°C). Grease a cast iron pan with the oil.
2. Whisk the eggs in a bowl.
3. Add the salt, olives, and mushrooms to the bowl with the whisked eggs and stir gently to combine.
4. Add the egg mixture to the pan. Top with feta cheese and bake for 20 minutes or until the frittata has set.
5. Garnish the frittata with the basil leaves and serve.

NUTRITION - AMOUNT PER SERVING

Calories	260	Sugar	1g
Fat	22g	Protein	14g
Carbs	2g	Cholesterol	380mg
Fiber	0g	Sodium	459mg

Pear

 5 Minutes

 1 Serving

INGREDIENTS

- 1 Pear

INSTRUCTIONS

1. Cut the pear in half lengthwise. Cut each half in half again and use a knife to remove the core.
2. Place all pieces in a bowl and enjoy!

NUTRITION - AMOUNT PER SERVING

Calories	101	Sugar	17g
Fat	0g	Protein	1g
Carbs	27g	Cholesterol	0mg
Fiber	6g	Sodium	2mg

Tuna Stuffed Pepper

 5 Minutes

 1 Serving

INGREDIENTS

- 1 can Tuna (drained)
- 2 tbsps Cream Cheese (regular)
- ½ stalk Green Onion (thinly sliced)
- 1 tbsp Parsley (chopped)
- 1 tsp Whole Grain Mustard
- 1 Red Bell Pepper (medium, halved)

INSTRUCTIONS

1. Mix the tuna, cream cheese, green onion, parsley, and mustard in a bowl.

2. Portion into red pepper halves and enjoy!

NUTRITION - AMOUNT PER SERVING

Calories	1267	Sugar	6g
Fat	11g	Protein	36g
Carbs	9g	Cholesterol	86mg
Fiber	3g	Sodium	570mg

Easy Home Salad

 10 Minutes

 1 Serving

INGREDIENTS

- 1 tbsp Extra Virgin Olive Oil
- 1 ½ tsps Red Wine Vinegar
- ⅛ head Green Lettuce (roughly chopped)
- ½ Tomato (medium, sliced)
- ¼ Cucumber (sliced)

INSTRUCTIONS

1. Combine the olive oil with the vinegar in a small bowl, whisking until well blended.
2. Place the remaining ingredients in a large bowl and drizzle with the dressing. Toss until well coated.

NUTRITION - AMOUNT PER SERVING

Calories	141	Sugar	1g
Fat	14g	Protein	1g
Carbs	5g	Cholesterol	0mg
Fiber	1g	Sodium	27mg

Poached Salmon, Artichokes & Sweet Potato

 15 Minutes

 1 Serving

INGREDIENTS

- 1 cup Vegetable Broth (low sodium)
- ½ Sweet Potato (large, diced)
- 1 Garlic (clove, chopped)
- 170 grams Salmon Fillet (skinless)
- ½ cup Artichoke Hearts (marinated, halved)
- 1 ½ stalks Green Onion (sliced)
- ¼ Lemon (juiced)
- Sea Salt & Black Pepper (to taste)

INSTRUCTIONS

1. Bring the broth to a boil in a deep pan with a lid. Add the potatoes and garlic. Cover and simmer for 5 minutes.
2. Add the salmon, artichokes, and green onions. Cover the pan again and cook for another 5 minutes or until the salmon is completely cooked.
3. Remove from the heat and stir in the lemon juice. Season with salt and pepper.
4. Serve in a bowl and enjoy!

NUTRITION - AMOUNT PER SERVING

Calories	325	Sugar	22g
Fat	9g	Protein	87mg
Carbs	8g	Cholesterol	7g
Fiber	41g	Sodium	671mg

REFER TO ORANGE ON PAGE 32 FOR QUANTITY AND NUTRITIONAL INFORMATION

Dinners

Baked Cod with Chickpeas & Tomatoes

 30 Minutes

 1 Serving

INGREDIENTS

- ½ cup Diced Tomatoes (from the can, with the juices)
- ½ cup Cherry Tomatoes
- ½ cup Chickpeas (cooked)
- ⅛ Yellow Onion (medium, diced)
- 1 Garlic (clove, minced)
- Sea Salt & Black Pepper (to taste)
- 1 Cod Fillet
- 1 ½ tsps Parsley (chopped)

INSTRUCTIONS

1. Preheat oven to 400°F (205°C).
2. Add the diced tomatoes, cherry tomatoes, chickpeas, onion, and garlic in an oven-safe dish. Stir the vegetable mixture and season with salt and pepper.
3. Place the dish in the oven and bake for 10 to 15 minutes. Before removing the dish from the oven, season the cod with a pinch of sea salt and black pepper.
4. Stir the vegetable mix, then arrange the cod fillets on top. Bake in the oven for another 10 to 12 minutes.
5. Sprinkle with parsley and enjoy!

NUTRITION - AMOUNT PER SERVING

Calories	374	Sugar	10g
Fat	4g	Protein	50g
Carbs	32g	Cholesterol	99mg
Fiber	9g	Sodium	157mg

Apple

 **2 Minutes**

 1 Serving

INGREDIENTS

- 1 Apple

INSTRUCTIONS

1. Slice into wedges or enjoy whole.

NUTRITION - AMOUNT PER SERVING

Calories	95	Sugar	19g
Fat	0g	Protein	0g
Carbs	25g	Cholesterol	0mg
Fiber	4g	Sodium	2mg

Chicken & Asparagus Pesto Pasta

 30 Minutes

 1 Serving

INGREDIENTS

- 75 grams Chicken Breast
- ½ cup Asparagus (ends trimmed)
- ¾ tsp Extra Virgin Olive Oil
- 70 grams Chickpea Pasta (dry)
- 1⅓ tbsps Pesto
- ¾ tsp Lemon Juice
- 2 ¼ tsps Parmigiano Reggiano Parmesan Cheese (finely grated)
- Sea Salt & Black Pepper (to taste)

INSTRUCTIONS

1. Preheat oven to 400°F (205°C). Line a baking tray with parchment paper.
2. Place the chicken and asparagus on the parchment paper and drizzle with olive oil.
3. Bake until the chicken is cooked, approximately 25 minutes.
4. Cut the chicken and asparagus into bite-size pieces when cool.
5. While the chicken is cooking, follow the packaging instructions to cook the pasta.
6. Mix the chicken, asparagus, pasta, pesto, lemon juice, and parmesan to assemble the pasta dish. Season with salt and pepper.

NUTRITION - AMOUNT PER SERVING

Calories	456	Sugar	9g
Fat	19g	Protein	36g
Carbs	44g	Cholesterol	48mg
Fiber	12g	Sodium	262mg

Blueberries

 2 Minutes

 1 Serving

INGREDIENTS

- 1 cup Blueberries

INSTRUCTIONS

1. Wash the berries and enjoy!

NUTRITION - AMOUNT PER SERVING

Calories	84	Sugar	115g
Fat	0g	Protein	1g
Carbs	21g	Cholesterol	0mg
Fiber	4g	Sodium	1mg

Baked Salmon with Broccoli & Quinoa

 20 Minutes

 1 Serving

INGREDIENTS

- 140 grams Salmon Fillet
- Sea Salt & Black Pepper (to taste)
- 1 cup Broccoli (sliced into small florets)
- 1 tbsp Extra Virgin Olive Oil
- ¼ cup Quinoa (uncooked)
- ⅓ cup Water
- ⅛ Lemon (sliced into wedges)

INSTRUCTIONS

1. Preheat oven to 450°F (232°C). Line a baking tray with parchment paper.
2. Season the salmon with sea salt and black pepper before placing the salmon on the baking tray.
3. Coat the broccoli florets in olive oil and season with sea salt and black pepper. Arrange the florets on the baking tray around the salmon.
4. Oven-bake the salmon and broccoli until the salmon flakes with a fork, approximately 15 minutes.
5. While the salmon cooks, combine the quinoa and water in a saucepan. When the water is boiling, cover it with a lid and reduce the heat to a gentle simmer for about 12 minutes or until all the water is absorbed.
6. Remove the quinoa from the heat once cooked and use a fork to fluff it up. Set it aside for later use.
7. Remove the salmon and broccoli from the oven and plate.
8. Serve with quinoa and a lemon wedge. Season with extra sea salt, black pepper, and olive oil.

NUTRITION - AMOUNT PER SERVING

Calories	494	Sugar	29g
Fat	23g	Protein	40g
Carbs	34g	Cholesterol	72mg
Fiber	5g	Sodium	145mg

Fresh Strawberries

 5 Minutes

 1 Serving

INGREDIENTS

- 1 cup Strawberries

INSTRUCTIONS

1. Wash strawberries under cold water and remove the stems. Dry well.
2. Slice and divide into bowls.

NUTRITION - AMOUNT PER SERVING

Calories	46	Sugar	7g
Fat	0g	Protein	1g
Carbs	11g	Cholesterol	0mg
Fiber	3g	Sodium	1mg

Beef & Chickpea Lettuce Wraps

 20 Minutes

 1 Serving

INGREDIENTS

- 1 tsp Extra Virgin Olive Oil
- 120 grams Extra Lean Ground Beef
- ⅛ tsp Garlic Powder
- ¹⁄₁₆ tsp Cumin
- Sea Salt & Black Pepper (to taste)
- ½ cup Chickpeas (cooked)
- ⅛ head Boston Lettuce (leaves pulled apart)

INSTRUCTIONS

1. In a large pan, heat the oil over a medium heat. Add the ground beef, garlic powder, cumin, salt, and pepper. Break up the beef as it cooks. Cook for 5 to 6 minutes or until it is almost cooked through.
2. Add the chickpeas to the beef and stir. Season with salt and pepper. Cook for another 4 to 5 minutes.
3. To assemble, divide the beef and chickpea mixture evenly between the lettuce leaves.

NUTRITION - AMOUNT PER SERVING

Calories	385	Sugar	4g
Fat	19g	Protein	31g
Carbs	23g	Cholesterol	77mg
Fiber	6g	Sodium	85mg

REFER TO BLUEBERRIES ON PAGE 46 FOR QUANTITY AND NUTRITIONAL INFORMATION

One Pan Tuna Steak & Bell Peppers

 25 Minutes

 1 Serving

INGREDIENTS

- 140 grams Tuna Steak
- 2 ¼ tsps Extra Virgin Olive Oil (divided)
- Sea Salt & Black Pepper (to taste)
- ¼ cup Shallots (thinly sliced)
- ½ Red Bell Pepper (medium, sliced)
- ½ Orange Bell Pepper (medium, sliced)
- 2 tbsps Almonds (roasted, finely chopped)
- ¼ cup Basil Leaves (chopped)

INSTRUCTIONS

1. Rub the tuna steaks with 1/3 oil and season with salt and pepper. Set aside.
2. Warm the remaining oil in a large, non-stick skillet over medium-high heat. Add the shallots and peppers to the skillet. Cook until the peppers start to brown, approximately 10 minutes, stirring occasionally.
3. Add the almonds and cook for 3 more minutes.
4. Add the basil, season to taste, and mix. Cover the pepper mixture and set aside.
5. Increase the heat to high and sear the tuna steaks for 2 to 3 minutes per side. The cooking time may vary based on the thickness of the tuna and your preferred level of doneness.
6. Serve the peppers and tuna on a plate and enjoy!

NUTRITION - AMOUNT PER SERVING

Calories	419	Sugar	6g
Fat	20g	Protein	41g
Carbs	20g	Cholesterol	55mg
Fiber	6g	Sodium	74mg

REFER TO GRAPES ON PAGE 36 FOR QUANTITY AND NUTRITIONAL INFORMATION

Salmon, Collard Greens & Cauliflower

 20 Minutes

 1 Serving

INGREDIENTS

- ¼ head Cauliflower (cut into florets)
- Sea Salt & Black Pepper (to taste)
- ¾ tsp Extra Virgin Olive Oil (divided)
- ½ Garlic (clove, large, minced)
- 170 grams Salmon Fillet
- 1 tbsp Water
- 1 ½ cups Collard Greens (thinly sliced)

INSTRUCTIONS

1. Boil the cauliflower in a large pot of water until tender, about 5 to 10 minutes. Drain the cauliflower and add salt and pepper to taste.
2. Meanwhile, add half of the oil to a large skillet over medium heat.
3. Add the garlic and salmon and cook for 4 minutes and then flip it.
4. Add the remaining oil, water, and collard greens to the skillet around the salmon. Season with salt and pepper. Cover and cook for 4 minutes or until the collard greens are softened and the salmon is cooked through.
5. Place the salmon, collard greens, and cauliflower on a plate and enjoy!

NUTRITION - AMOUNT PER SERVING

Calories	309	Sugar	3g
Fat	12g	Protein	42g
Carbs	11g	Cholesterol	87mg
Fiber	5g	Sodium	186mg

REFER TO KIWI ON PAGE 34 FOR QUANTITY AND NUTRITIONAL INFORMATION

Lemon & Asparagus Chicken Skillet

 25 Minutes

 1 Serving

INGREDIENTS

- 113 grams Chicken Breast (skinless, boneless, cubed)
- ⅛ tsp Sea Salt (divided, to taste)
- 1 cup Butternut Squash (peeled, cubed)
- 1 cup Asparagus (trimmed, chopped)
- 1 ½ tsps Water
- ¾ tsp Lemon Juice (to taste)

INSTRUCTIONS

1. Heat a large skillet over medium heat.
2. Add the chicken to the skillet. Cook for 7 to 8 minutes or until cooked through. Season with half of the salt. Set aside.
3. Add the squash and remaining salt. Cook, stirring occasionally, for 5 minutes. Add the asparagus and water, cover with a lid, and steam for 5 minutes. Add more water if needed.
4. Return the chicken to the skillet. Stir and heat for 1 minute. Serve on a plate, squeeze lemon juice over the top, and enjoy!

NUTRITION - AMOUNT PER SERVING

Calories	226	Sugar	6g
Fat	3g	Protein	30g
Carbs	22g	Cholesterol	82mg
Fiber	6g	Sodium	354mg

REFER TO APPLE ON PAGE 44 FOR QUANTITY AND NUTRITIONAL INFORMATION

Snacks

Grilled Apricots with Yogurt & Pistachios

 15 Minutes

 1 Serving

INGREDIENTS

- 2 Apricots
  (halved, pits removed)
- 2 tbsps Plain Greek
  Yogurt
- 1 tbsp Pistachios
  (chopped)

INSTRUCTIONS

1. Preheat a grill skillet. Place the apricot halves on the skillet face down and cook for 7 minutes, until softened, and they have grill marks.
2. Add apricots to a plate, face up, and top with yogurt and pistachios.

NUTRITION - AMOUNT PER SERVING

Calories	99	Sugar	8g
Fat	4g	Protein	5g
Carbs	11g	Cholesterol	4mg
Fiber	2g	Sodium	18mg

Lemon Dill Yogurt Dip with Carrots & Celery

 10 Minutes

 1 Serving

INGREDIENTS

- ½ cup Plain Greek Yogurt
- ¼ Lemon (juiced)
- 1 tbsp Fresh Dill (finely chopped)
- 1 Carrot (medium, peeled, cut into sticks)
- 1 stalk Celery (cut into sticks)

INSTRUCTIONS

1. Mix the yogurt, lemon juice, and chopped dill in a small bowl. Serve with carrot and celery sticks.

NUTRITION - AMOUNT PER SERVING

Calories	124	Sugar	12g
Fat	3g	Protein	7g
Carbs	14g	Cholesterol	17mg
Fiber	2g	Sodium	145mg

Snap Peas & Hummus

 5 Minutes

 1 Servings

INGREDIENTS

- 1 cup Snap Peas (trimmed)
- ⅓ cup Hummus

INSTRUCTIONS

1. Serve the snap peas with the hummus.

NUTRITION - AMOUNT PER SERVING

Calories	225	Sugar	4g
Fat	15g	Protein	8g
Carbs	19g	Cholesterol	0mg
Fiber	7g	Sodium	355mg

Grapes & Almonds

 5 Minutes

 1 Serving

INGREDIENTS

- 1 cup Grapes
- ¼ cup Almonds

INSTRUCTIONS

1. Combine grapes and almonds in a bowl.

NUTRITION - AMOUNT PER SERVING

Calories	269	Sugar	17g
Fat	18g	Protein	8g
Carbs	23g	Cholesterol	0mg
Fiber	5g	Sodium	2mg

Pistachio Trail Mix

 5 Minutes

 1 Serving

INGREDIENTS

- 2 ⅔ tbsps Pistachios (shells removed)
- 2 ⅔ tbsps Goji Berries
- 1 ⅓ tbsps Dark Chocolate Chips
- 2 ⅔ tbsps Cashews

INSTRUCTIONS

1. Add the pistachios, goji berries, chocolate chips, and cashews to a jar. Shake until mixed well.

NUTRITION - AMOUNT PER SERVING

Calories	419	Sugar	19g
Fat	27g	Protein	11g
Carbs	35g	Cholesterol	0mg
Fiber	5g	Sodium	48mg

Coconut Yogurt, Strawberries & Blackberries

 5 Minutes

 1 Serving

INGREDIENTS

- ½ cup Unsweetened Coconut Yogurt
- ¼ cup Strawberries (chopped)
- 1 cup Blackberries

INSTRUCTIONS

1. Add the coconut yogurt, strawberries, and blackberries to a bowl.

NUTRITION - AMOUNT PER SERVING

Calories	129	Sugar	9g
Fat	4g	Protein	3g
Carbs	23g	Cholesterol	0mg
Fiber	10g	Sodium	27mg

Yogurt & Fresh Apricot

 5 Minutes

 1 Serving

INGREDIENTS

- 1 cup Unsweetened Coconut Yogurt
- 1 Apricot (pitted, sliced)
- 1 tsp Ground Flax Seed
- 1 ½ tbsps Walnuts (chopped)

INSTRUCTIONS

1. Add the yogurt and apricot to a bowl. Place the flax seed and walnuts on top.

NUTRITION - AMOUNT PER SERVING

Calories	212	Sugar	5g
Fat	15g	Protein	4g
Carbs	18g	Cholesterol	0mg
Fiber	5g	Sodium	50mg

WEEK 2

7-Days Meal Plan

MONDAY

BREAKFAST
Warm Apple Chia Pudding

LUNCH
Chicken & Zucchini Skillet, Fresh Strawberries

DINNER
Lemon Garlic Chicken & Green Beans, Pineapple

SNACKS
Tuna with Bell Pepper

TUESDAY

BREAKFAST
Green Pancakes

LUNCH
Chicken, Lettuce & Tomato Egg Wrap, Baked Sweet Potato

DINNER
Turmeric Chicken with Brown Rice

SNACKS
Pecans & Blueberries

WEDNESDAY

BREAKFAST
Banana Oat Pancakes

LUNCH
Lemon & Dill Baked Sole, Peach

DINNER
Beef & Cauliflower Skillet, Grapes

SNACKS
Cottage Cheese & Orange

THURSDAY

BREAKFAST
Egg in a Hole, Kiwi Green Smoothie

LUNCH
Garlic Shrimp & Snow Pea Shoots, Banana

DINNER
One Pan Tamari Beef & Vegetables, Apple

SNACKS
Bell Peppers with Hummus

FRIDAY

BREAKFAST
Avocado Toast with Poached Egg

LUNCH
Tuna Arugula Salad, Kiwi

DINNER
Pasta with Spinach & Turkey, Orange

SNACKS
Cottage Cheese with Blueberries

SATURDAY

BREAKFAST
Carrot & Parsley Omelet

LUNCH
Lemon Oregano Chicken, Tomato Avocado Salad

DINNER
Salsa Steamed Cod, Pineapple

SNACKS
Peach Yogurt Parfait

SUNDAY

BREAKFAST
Cream Cheese Eggs & Spinach

LUNCH
Salmon with Rice & Broccoli, Fresh Strawberries

DINNER
Pesto Tuna & Pea Quinoa Salad, Grapes

SNACKS
Tuna & Kale Chips

Shopping List

FRUITS

2 Apples
1 Avocado
2 Bananas
1 ¼ cups Blueberries
2 cups Grapes
3 Kiwis
½ Lemon
1 ¾ tbsps Juice
½ Lime
2 Navel Oranges
1 ½ Peaches
3 cups Pineapple
2 cups Strawberries

SEEDS, NUTS & SPICES

Sea Salt & Black Pepper
¼ cup Chia Seeds
¼ tsp Cinnamon
½ tsp Cumin
⅓ tsp Garlic Powder
1 ½ tsps Ground Flax Seeds
¾ tsp Italian Seasoning
1 ⅛ tsps Oregano
⅓ tsp Paprika
⅓ cup Pecans
⅓ tsp Turmeric

FROZEN

1 cup Cauliflower Rice
½ cup Frozen Peas

VEGETABLES

2 cups Arugula
1 ½ cups Asparagus
5 ¾ cups Baby Spinach
1 cup Bok Choy
1 cup Broccoli
4 Carrots
2 tbsps Cilantro
1 tbsp Fresh Dill
3 ⅓ Garlic
1 ½ cups Green Beans
2 cups Kale Leaves
1 ½ stalks Green Onion
2 tbsps Parsley
1 ¼ Red Bell Peppers
⅓ cup Red Onion
1 leaf Romaine Lettuce
3 cups Snow Pea Shoots
1 Sweet Potato
1 ¼ Tomatoes
½ Yellow Bell Pepper
¼ Yellow Onion
1 ½ Zucchini

PANTRY STAPLES

1 tbsp Almond Butter
½ cup Granola
⅔ cup Brown Rice
2 ⅔ tbsps Chicken Broth
¼ cup Quinoa
¼ cup Salsa
2 cans Tuna
2 tbsps Vegetable Broth
½ cup White Navy Beans
60 grams Whole Wheat
   Penne

BAKING

1 tsp Baking Powder
½ cup Oat Flour

BREAD, FISH, MEAT & CHEESE

150 grams Chicken Breast
50 grams Chicken Breast
   (cooked)
263 grams Chicken Thighs
1 Cod Fillet
2 ½ tbsps Cream Cheese
   (regular)
310 grams Extra Lean
   Ground Beef
113 grams Extra Lean
   Ground Chicken
113 grams Extra Lean
   Ground Turkey
2 tbsps Feta Cheese
170 grams Salmon Fillet
125 grams Shrimp
113 grams Sole Fillet
2 slices Whole Grain Bread

CONDIMENTS & OILS

1 tbsp Apple Cider Vinegar
⅔ cup Extra Virgin Olive Oil
1 tbsp Pesto
1 ¼ tbsps Tamari

FRIDGE

1 tbsp Butter
1 ½ cups Cottage Cheese
8 ½ Eggs
¼ cup Hummus
¼ cup Oat Milk
⅔ cup Soy Milk
2 ¼ cups Unsweetened
   Almond Milk
⅔ cup Unsweetened
   Coconut Yogurt

Warm Apple Chia Pudding

 10 Minutes

 1 Serving

INGREDIENTS

- 3 tbsps Chia Seeds
- ¾ cup Unsweetened Almond Milk
- ¼ tsp Cinnamon
- 1 Apple (cored and diced)
- 2 tbsps Pecans
- 1 tbsp Almond Butter

INSTRUCTIONS

1. Over a medium-low heat, whisk the almond milk, chia seeds, and cinnamon in a small pot.
2. Stir until the mixture is hot and has thickened, about 5 to 7 minutes.
3. Add to a bowl and top with apples, pecans, and almond butter.

NUTRITION - AMOUNT PER SERVING

Calories	472	Sugar	20g
Fat	31g	Protein	12g
Carbs	46g	Cholesterol	0mg
Fiber	20g	Sodium	129mg

Green Pancakes

 20 Minutes

 1 Serving

INGREDIENTS

- ½ cup Oats
- ½ cup Baby Spinach (packed)
- ¼ cup Oat Milk (unsweetened, plain)
- ⅓ cup Unsweetened Apples Sauce
- ½ Egg (large)
- ½ tsp Baking Powder
- 1 ½ tsps Extra Virgin Olive Oil

INSTRUCTIONS

1. Pour the oats into an electric blender and blend until a flour consistency is reached, about 30 seconds. Add the baby spinach, milk, apple sauce, egg, and baking powder. Blend until smooth.
2. In a nonstick pan heat the oil. Add 1/4 cup of the batter at a time and cook for 2 to 3 minutes per side over a medium heat.
3. Transfer the pancakes to an oven-proof dish and keep warm. Repeat until all the batter has been used.
4. Plate the pancakes and enjoy!

NUTRITION - AMOUNT PER SERVING

Calories	322	Sugar	11g
Fat	13g	Protein	10g
Carbs	43g	Cholesterol	93mg
Fiber	6g	Sodium	321mg

Banana Oat Pancakes

 15 Minutes

 1 Serving

INGREDIENTS

- ½ cup Oat Flour
- ½ tsp Baking Powder
- 1 ½ tsps Ground Flax Seed
- ¹⁄₁₆ tsp Sea Salt
- ½ Banana
  (medium, mashed)
- ⅔ cup Soy Milk
- ¾ tsp Extra Virgin Olive Oil
- 1 Egg

INSTRUCTIONS

1. Mix together the flour, baking powder, ground flaxseed, and salt in a mixing bowl.
2. Add the mashed banana, beaten egg, and soy milk to the bowl. Stir until well combined.
3. Lightly grease a large non-stick skillet with oil and warm over a medium heat.
4. Add 1/4 cup of the banana pancake batter to a skillet and cook until bubbles form on the surface. Flip the pancake and cook for a further 1 to 2 minutes. Repeat with the remaining batter.
5. To serve, plate and top with maple syrup, if desired.

NUTRITION - AMOUNT PER SERVING

Calories	485	Sugar	13g
Fat	16g	Protein	23g
Carbs	63g	Cholesterol	186mg
Fiber	9g	Sodium	539mg

66

Egg in a Hole

 10 Minutes

 1 Serving

INGREDIENTS

- 1 slice Whole Grain Bread
- 1 tsp Extra Virgin Olive Oil
- 1 Egg (medium)

INSTRUCTIONS

1. Press a cookie cutter or cup's rim into the middle of your slice of bread. Remove the cut-out and set aside.
2. Heat all the olive oil in a small non-stick pan over a medium heat.
3. Toast the bread and the cut-out for about 2 minutes.
4. Flip the bread and cut-out, then crack the egg directly into the hole. Place a lid on the pan and lower the heat.
5. Cook for 4 to 5 minutes or until your desired doneness is reached.
6. Transfer to a plate and dip the bread cut-out into the egg.

NUTRITION - AMOUNT PER SERVING

Calories	221	Sugar	3g
Fat	11g	Protein	12g
Carbs	18g	Cholesterol	186mg
Fiber	3g	Sodium	228mg

Kiwi Green Smoothie

 5 Minutes

 1 Serving

INGREDIENTS

- 1 Kiwi (small, peeled)
- ½ Banana (frozen)
- 1 tbsp Chia Seeds
- 1 ¼ cups Baby Spinach
- 1 cup Water
- 2 Ice Cubes

INSTRUCTIONS

1. Add all the above ingredients to a blender. Once a smooth consistency is reached, pour the mixture into a glass and enjoy the refreshing taste!

NUTRITION - AMOUNT PER SERVING

Calories	160	Sugar	114g
Fat	4g	Protein	5g
Carbs	30g	Cholesterol	0mg
Fiber	8g	Sodium	39mg

Avocado Toast with Poached Egg

 15 Minutes

 1 Serving

INGREDIENTS

- 1 slice Whole Grain Bread
- ½ Avocado
- Sea Salt & Black Pepper (to taste)
- 1 Egg
- 1 tbsp Apple Cider Vinegar
- ⅛ tsp Sea Salt

INSTRUCTIONS

1. Toast the bread.
2. Cut the avocado in half, remove the pit, and cut it into fine slices. Layer the avocado on the toast, and season with salt and pepper.
3. Crack the egg into a small bowl.
4. On your stovetop, bring a pot of water to a rolling boil. Add sea salt and vinegar to the water. Begin stirring with a spoon to create a whirlpool. Carefully add the egg to the whirlpool and cook for 3 to 4 minutes.
5. Remove the cooked poached egg with a slotted spoon carefully.
6. Place the egg onto paper towel to soak up the excess liquid.
7. Place the egg on the top of your avocado toast and season with sea salt and pepper.

NUTRITION - AMOUNT PER SERVING

Calories	345	Sugar	4g
Fat	21g	Protein	14g
Carbs	27g	Cholesterol	186mg
Fiber	10g	Sodium	531mg

Carrot & Parsley Omelet

 10 Minutes

 1 Serving

INGREDIENTS

- 1 tbsp Extra Virgin Olive Oil
- 2 Eggs
- 1 cup Grated Carrot
- 2 tbsps Parsley (finely chopped)
- Sea Salt & Black Pepper (to taste)

INSTRUCTIONS

1. In a small non-stick pan warm the olive oil over a medium heat.
2. In a small bowl, beat the eggs, then mix in the grated carrot and chopped parsley. Season the omelet mixture with salt and freshly ground black pepper.
3. Add the omelet mixture to the pan. Cook for about 5 minutes or until almost set. Flip the omelet and cook for a further 2 to 3 minutes.
4. Remove from heat, plate, and enjoy!

NUTRITION - AMOUNT PER SERVING

Calories	310	Sugar	6g
Fat	23g	Protein	14g
Carbs	12g	Cholesterol	372mg
Fiber	3g	Sodium	222mg

Cream Cheese Eggs & Spinach

 10 Minutes

 1 Serving

INGREDIENTS

- 2 Eggs
- 1 ½ tbsps Cream Cheese, Regular
- 1 ½ cups Unsweetened Almond Milk
- Sea Salt & Black Pepper (to taste)
- 1 tbsp Extra Virgin Olive Oil (divided)
- 2 cups Baby Spinach

INSTRUCTIONS

1. Crack the eggs into a medium bowl carefully and whisk well. Add the cream cheese and milk. Season with salt and pepper. Whisk again and set aside.
2. Warm half the oil in a medium non-stick skillet over medium-low heat. Add the spinach and sauté until wilted, about 1 to 2 minutes. Remove the spinach and set it aside.
3. Using the same skillet over medium-low heat, heat the remaining oil. Pour in the egg mixture and continuously stir until cooked to the desired doneness.
4. Plate the eggs and top with spinach.

NUTRITION - AMOUNT PER SERVING

Calories	386	Sugar	1g
Fat	33g	Protein	17g
Carbs	5g	Cholesterol	392mg
Fiber	3g	Sodium	529mg

Lunches

Chicken & Zucchini Skillet

 5 Minutes

 1 Serving

INGREDIENTS

- 1 tbsp Extra Virgin Olive Oil (divided)
- 1 Carrot (large, diced)
- 1 Zucchini (large, diced)
- 1/16 tsp Sea Salt (to taste)
- 113 grams Extra Lean Ground Chicken
- 1/8 tsp Garlic Powder
- 1 cup Baby Spinach

INSTRUCTIONS

1. Warm half the oil in a non-stick skillet over medium-high heat. Cook the carrot and zucchini until fork-tender, about 5 minutes. Transfer the cooked vegetables to a bowl. Season with sea salt and black pepper.
2. Heat the remaining olive oil in the used skillet. Add the ground chicken and cook for about 10 minutes, breaking it up as it cooks. Drain any excess liquid.
3. Stir in the garlic powder, spinach, and cooked veggies. Once the spinach is wilted and the liquid is mostly absorbed, serve in a bowl and enjoy!

NUTRITION - AMOUNT PER SERVING

Calories	348	Sugar	8g
Fat	24g	Protein	24g
Carbs	13g	Cholesterol	98mg
Fiber	4g	Sodium	298mg

REFER TO STRAWBERRIES ON PAGE 48 FOR QUANTITY AND NUTRITIONAL INFORMATION

Chicken, Lettuce & Tomato Egg Wrap

 15 Minutes

 1 Serving

INGREDIENTS

- 1 Egg
- ¹⁄₁₆ tsp Sea Salt
- ¼ tsp Extra Virgin Olive Oil
- 1 leave Romaine (large, whole)
- ¼ Tomato (sliced)
- 50 grams Chicken Breast (cooked, sliced)

INSTRUCTIONS

1. Whisk the eggs and salt together in a mixing bowl.
2. Add the olive oil to a small non-stick pan and heat using a medium heat setting.
3. Pour the beaten eggs into the pan. To ensure the egg is distributed evenly, tilt the pan in a circular motion. Allow it to cook for 60 to 90 seconds, or until it is fully set and easily released from the pan.
4. Then, flip the egg and continue cooking for 30 to 60 seconds until cooked through.
5. To serve, layer the lettuce, tomato, and cooked chicken on the egg wrap and roll or fold together.

NUTRITION - AMOUNT PER SERVING

Calories	166	Sugar	1g
Fat	8g	Protein	22g
Carbs	2g	Cholesterol	238mg
Fiber	1g	Sodium	258mg

Baked Sweet Potato

 20 Minutes

 1 Serving

INGREDIENTS

- 1 Sweet Potato (medium)
- ⅛ tsp Sea Salt
- 1 tbsp Extra Virgin Olive Oil
- ½ tsp Oregano
- ⅛ tsp Black Pepper

INSTRUCTIONS

1. Preheat oven to 350°F (180°C). Coat a non-stick baking tray with olive oil.
2. Wash and peel the potatoes and cut into medium-sized chunks.
3. Place the potato chunks on the baking tray and coat with olive oil by turning each chunk. Sprinkle the potatoes with oregano, sea salt, and black pepper.
4. Place the potatoes into the oven and cook until soft inside and slightly crisp and brown on the outside, about 45 minutes to 1 hour.

NUTRITION - AMOUNT PER SERVING

Calories	233	Sugar	5g
Fat	14g	Protein	2g
Carbs	27g	Cholesterol	0mg
Fiber	4g	Sodium	367mg

Lemon & Dill Baked Sole

 15 Minutes

 1 Serving

INGREDIENTS

- 1 tbsp Extra Virgin Olive Oil
- ¼ Lemon (divided)
- 1 ½ tsps Fresh Dill (chopped)
- Sea Salt & Black Pepper (to taste)
- 113 grams Sole Fillet (boneless)
- 1 ½ cups Asparagus (woody ends trimmed)

INSTRUCTIONS

1. Preheat oven to 350°F (180°C). Line a baking tray with parchment paper.
2. Combine the olive oil and juice of half the lemon, dill, salt, and pepper in a small bowl.
3. Arrange the sole and asparagus onto the baking sheet and coat evenly in the lemon-dill mixture. Top with the remaining lemon cut into slices. Bake for 10 to 15 minutes or until the fish is opaque and the asparagus is tender.

NUTRITION - AMOUNT PER SERVING

Calories	242	Sugar	4g
Fat	16g	Protein	19g
Carbs	9g	Cholesterol	51mg
Fiber	4g	Sodium	340mg

Peach

 5 Minutes

 1 Serving

INGREDIENTS

- 1 Peach

INSTRUCTIONS

1. Wash and enjoy whole or sliced.

NUTRITION - AMOUNT PER SERVING

Calories	59	Sugar	13g
Fat	0g	Protein	1g
Carbs	14g	Cholesterol	0mg
Fiber	2g	Sodium	0mg

Garlic Shrimp & Snow Pea Shoots

 10 Minutes

 1 Serving

INGREDIENTS

- 1 tbsp Extra Virgin Olive Oil
- 1 Garlic Clove (minced)
- 3 cups Snow Pea Shoots
- 125 grams Shrimp (cooked)
- Sea Salt & Black Pepper (to taste)
- ½ tsp Lemon Juice (to taste)

INSTRUCTIONS

1. Warm a pan with the olive oil over a medium heat. Add the garlic, snow pea leaves, shrimp, salt and pepper. Cook for about 4 to 5 minutes, or until the leaves are deep green and the shrimp is warmed through.
2. Plate your meal, squeeze lemon juice over the top, and enjoy!

NUTRITION - AMOUNT PER SERVING

Calories	322	Sugar	9g
Fat	14g	Protein	32g
Carbs	19g	Cholesterol	205mg
Fiber	6g	Sodium	153mg

Banana

 1 Minute 1 Serving

INGREDIENTS

- 1 Banana

INSTRUCTIONS

1. Peel and enjoy!

NUTRITION - AMOUNT PER SERVING	
Calories	105
Fat	0g
Carbs	27g
Fiber	3g
Sugar	14g
Protein	1g
Cholesterol	0mg
Sodium	1mg

Cherries

 2 Minutes 1 Serving

INGREDIENTS

- 1 cup Fresh Cherries

INSTRUCTIONS

1. Wash the cherries and place them in a bowl.

NUTRITION - AMOUNT PER SERVING	
Calories	97
Fat	0g
Carbs	25g
Fiber	3g
Sugar	20g
Protein	2g
Cholesterol	0mg
Sodium	0mg

Tuna Arugula Salad

 10 Minutes

 1 Serving

INGREDIENTS

- 1 ¼ tbsps Extra Virgin Olive Oil
- 2 ¼ tsps Lemon Juice
- 1 ½ tsps Fresh Dill (chopped)
- Sea Salt & Black Pepper (to taste)
- 2 cups Arugula
- ½ cup White Navy Beans
- 2 tbsps Red Onion (sliced)
- ½ can Tuna (drained, broken into chunks)

INSTRUCTIONS

1. Combine the oil, lemon juice, dill, salt, and pepper in a small bowl. Set the dressing aside.
2. Add the arugula, white beans, and red onion onto a plate. Top with tuna chunks and drizzle with the dressing.

NUTRITION - AMOUNT PER SERVING

Calories	368	Sugar	2g
Fat	19g	Protein	25g
Carbs	28g	Cholesterol	30mg
Fiber	11g	Sodium	216mg

REFER TO KIWIS ON PAGE 34 FOR QUANTITY AND NUTRITIONAL INFORMATION

Lemon Oregano Chicken

 30 Minutes

 1 Serving

INGREDIENTS

- 113 grams Chicken Thighs (bone-in, skin removed)
- ½ Garlic (clove, minced)
- ¼ Lemon (zest and juice divided)
- ⅔ tsp Oregano
- ⅛ tsp Sea Salt

INSTRUCTIONS

1. Preheat oven to 400°F (204°C). Line a baking tray with parchment paper.
2. Add the garlic, lemon zest, half the lemon juice, oregano, and salt to a large bowl. Add the chicken and coat the thighs evenly with the seasoning.
3. Transfer the seasoned chicken thighs onto the parchment paper and cook for about 25 minutes until thoroughly cooked. Remove the tray from the oven.
4. Plate the chicken and drizzle with the remaining lemon juice. If needed, season with additional salt.

NUTRITION - AMOUNT PER SERVING

Calories	144	Sugar	0g
Fat	5g	Protein	22g
Carbs	2g	Cholesterol	107mg
Fiber	0g	Sodium	403mg

Tomato Avocado Salad

 10 Minutes

 1 Serving

INGREDIENTS

- 1 Tomato (medium, chopped)
- ½ Avocado (medium, chopped)
- 2 tbsps Red Onion (sliced)
- 2 tbsps Feta Cheese (cubed)
- ½ Lime (juiced)
- Sea Salt & Black Pepper (to taste)

INSTRUCTIONS

1. Arrange the tomato, avocado, and red onion in a bowl.
2. Top with feta cheese, drizzle with lime juice, and season with salt and pepper.

NUTRITION - AMOUNT PER SERVING

Calories	3242	Sugar	2g
Fat	19g	Protein	6g
Carbs	17g	Cholesterol	17mg
Fiber	8g	Sodium	268mg

Salmon with Rice & Broccoli

 30 Minutes

 1 Serving

INGREDIENTS

- ¼ cup Brown Rice (dry)
- 170 grams Salmon Fillet
- Sea Salt & Black Pepper (to taste)
- ¾ tsp Extra Virgin Olive Oil
- 1 cup Broccoli (florets)

INSTRUCTIONS

1. Cook the brown rice following the directions on the packet.
2. Meanwhile, warm the olive oil in a non-stick pan or skillet over a medium heat setting.
3. To ensure the salmon is dry, pat it with a paper towel. Once dry, completely season the salmon with salt and pepper.
4. Add the salmon to the non-stick pan or skillet and cook each side for 4 to 6 minutes until thoroughly cooked.
5. Meanwhile, steam the broccoli by adding the florets to a steamer basket. Cover with a lid and steam over the boiling water for about 5 minutes until tender.
6. Place the rice, salmon, and broccoli on a plate to serve.

NUTRITION - AMOUNT PER SERVING

Calories	453	Sugar	2g
Fat	13g	Protein	44g
Carbs	41g	Cholesterol	87mg
Fiber	4g	Sodium	165mg

REFER TO STRAWBERRIES ON PAGE 48 FOR QUANTITY AND NUTRITIONAL INFORMATION

Dinners

Lemon Garlic Chicken & Green Beans

 20 Minutes

 1 Serving

INGREDIENTS

- 150 grams Chicken Thighs (boneless, skinless)
- ⅓ tsp Paprika
- Sea Salt & Black Pepper (to taste)
- 1 tbsp Butter (divided)
- 1 cup Green Beans (trimmed, fresh)
- 1 ⅓ Garlic (clove, minced)
- 2 ⅔ tbsps Chicken Broth
- 2 tsps Lemon Juice

INSTRUCTIONS

1. Season the chicken thighs with paprika, sea salt, and black pepper.
2. Add ⅔ of the butter to a skillet or non-stick pan and melt over medium-high heat.
3. Add the chicken to the skillet or pan and cook each side for 5 to 6 minutes until thoroughly cooked. Remove the chicken from the pan.
4. Reduce the heat to low and add the remaining butter, green beans, and garlic, and cook for 4 minutes, stirring occasionally.
5. Add the chicken broth and lemon juice. Cook for about 5 minutes until the liquid is reduced.
6. Add the chicken back to the pan until warm before plating.

NUTRITION - AMOUNT PER SERVING

Calories	329	Sugar	3g
Fat	18g	Protein	32g
Carbs	10g	Cholesterol	173mg
Fiber	4g	Sodium	306mg

Pineapple

 5 Minutes

 1 Serving

INGREDIENTS

- 1 ½ cups Pineapple

INSTRUCTIONS

1. Slice into cubes and serve in a bowl.

NUTRITION - AMOUNT PER SERVING

Calories	124	Sugar	24g
Fat	0g	Protein	1g
Carbs	32g	Cholesterol	0mg
Fiber	3g	Sodium	2mg

Turmeric Chicken with Brown Rice

 30 Minutes

 1 Serving

INGREDIENTS

- ⅓ cup Brown Rice (dry, uncooked)
- 150 grams Chicken Breast (skinless and boneless)
- 1 tbsp Extra Virgin Olive Oil
- ⅓ tsp Turmeric
- Sea Salt & Black Pepper (to taste)

INSTRUCTIONS

1. Preheat oven to 400°F (204°C). Line a baking tray with parchment paper.
2. Following the directions on the packet, cook the brown rice.
3. Mix the avocado oil, turmeric, salt and pepper in a bowl. Toss the chicken in the mix, and when coated, transfer to the baking tray.
4. While the rice cooks, bake the chicken for 25 to 30 minutes or until cooked.
5. To plate, slice the chicken and serve on top of the rice.

NUTRITION - AMOUNT PER SERVING

Calories	530	Sugar	10g
Fat	19g	Protein	39g
Carbs	48g	Cholesterol	110mg
Fiber	2g	Sodium	71mg

Beef & Cauliflower Skillet

 20 Minutes

 1 Serving

INGREDIENTS

- 140 grams Extra Lean Ground Beef
- ¼ Yellow Onion (chopped)
- ½ Zucchini (halved lengthwise, seeds removed, and diced)
- 1 cup Cauliflower Rice
- ½ tsp Italian Seasoning
- ¼ tsp Garlic Powder
- ¼ tsp Sea Salt
- ¾ tsp Lemon Juice (optional)

INSTRUCTIONS

1. Warm a large skillet over medium heat. Place the beef in the skillet, breaking it up with a spatula as it cooks. Once the beef is fully cooked and no longer pink, transfer it to a bowl. If necessary, drain any excess fat from the skillet before continuing.
2. Without rinsing the skillet, add the onion and sauté for 2 to 3 minutes until it becomes translucent. Add the zucchini and cook until soft, 3 to 5 minutes. If the zucchini or onions start to stick, add a few drops of water to the pan to help loosen them.
3. Add the cooked beef and cauliflower rice to the skillet. Season all with Italian seasoning, garlic powder, and salt and stir to combine. Cook for 2 to 3 minutes until the beef is hot and the cauliflower is cooked to the desired doneness.
4. Remove the skillet from the heat. Stir in the optional lemon juice and season with additional salt to taste before serving.

NUTRITION - AMOUNT PER SERVING

Calories	311	Sugar	7g
Fat	15g	Protein	32g
Carbs	11g	Cholesterol	92mg
Fiber	4g	Sodium	718mg

REFER TO GRAPES ON PAGE 36 FOR QUANTITY AND NUTRITIONAL INFORMATION

One Pan Tamari Beef & Vegetables

 20 Minutes

 1 Serving

INGREDIENTS

- 170 grams Extra Lean Ground Beef
- ¼ Red Bell Pepper (diced)
- 1 ½ stalks Green Onion (chopped)
- ½ cup Green Beans (chopped)
- 1 cup Bok Choy (chopped)
- 1 ¼ tbsps Tamari

INSTRUCTIONS

1. Over a medium heat setting, heat a large, non-stick pan or skillet.
2. Breaking up the ground beef as you add it to the pan. Once the beef has browned and cooked, drain any excess fat from the pan.
3. Add the green onion, green beans and peppers to the pan and continue to cook for 5 to s6 minutes stirring regularly until the vegetables have softened.
4. Add the bok choy and tamari and cook for 2 to 3 minutes more until the bok choy is wilted and tender. Season with additional tamari if needed then serve.

NUTRITION - AMOUNT PER SERVING

Calories	350	Sugar	5g
Fat	17g	Protein	39g
Carbs	9g	Cholesterol	111mg
Fiber	3g	Sodium	1422mg

REFER TO APPLE ON PAGE 44 FOR QUANTITY AND NUTRITIONAL INFORMATION

Pasta with Spinach & Turkey

 **20 Minutes**

 **1 Serving**

INGREDIENTS

- 60 grams Whole Wheat Penne
- 1 ½ tsps Extra Virgin Olive Oil (divided)
- 113 grams Extra Lean Ground Turkey
- ¼ tsp Italian Seasoning
- ⅛ tsp Sea Salt
- 1 cup Baby Spinach

INSTRUCTIONS

1. Cook the penne pasta according to the packaging directions.
2. Meanwhile, in a large pan, heat half the oil over a medium heat setting. Add the ground turkey to the pan. Break it up with a spatula as it cooks. Stir in Italian seasoning, salt and spinach and cook until spinach has wilted.
3. Add the cooked pasta and remaining olive oil to the skillet and combine with the turkey and spinach.
4. Plate and season with sea salt if needed.

NUTRITION - AMOUNT PER SERVING

Calories	438	Sugar	2g
Fat	17g	Protein	28g
Carbs	44g	Cholesterol	84mg
Fiber	7g	Sodium	397mg

REFER TO ORANGE ON PAGE 32 FOR QUANTITY AND NUTRITIONAL INFORMATION

Salsa Steamed Cod

 15 Minutes

 1 Serving

INGREDIENTS

- 1 ½ tsps Extra Virgin Olive Oil
- 2 tbsps Red Onion (finely chopped)
- ½ Garlic (clove, large, minced)
- ½ tsp Cumin
- 2 tbsps Vegetable Broth
- ¼ cup Salsa
- 2 tbsps Cilantro (divided)
- 1 Cod Fillet

INSTRUCTIONS

1. Warm the oil in a large pot with a lid and add the onion and cook until translucent, about 4 minutes.
2. Add the garlic and cumin to the onion and cook until the onion mix becomes fragrant, about another minute.
3. Stir in the vegetable broth and salsa. Bring the salsa mixture to a simmer and cook for about 5 minutes. Stir in half of the cilantro.
4. Place the cod fillet in the pot and cover with the lid. Cook for about 6 to 7 minutes until cooked.
5. Plate the cod and sauce and top with the remaining cilantro.

NUTRITION - AMOUNT PER SERVING

Calories	284	Sugar	4g
Fat	9g	Protein	43g
Carbs	7g	Cholesterol	99mg
Fiber	2g	Sodium	673mg

REFER TO PINEAPPLE ON PAGE 84 FOR QUANTITY AND NUTRITIONAL INFORMATION

Pesto Tuna & Pea Quinoa Salad

 20 Minutes

 1 Serving

INGREDIENTS

- ¼ cup Quinoa (uncooked)
- ½ cup Water
- ½ can Tuna
  (drained, broken into chunks)
- ½ cup Frozen Peas (thawed)
- 1 tbsp Pesto

INSTRUCTIONS

1. Add the quinoa and water to a pot. Bring to a boil over a high heat setting. Reduce to a simmer and cover for 12 to 15 minutes, or until all water is absorbed. Remove lid and fluff with a fork.
2. Boil the peas according to the package instructions.
3. Add the tuna, cooked peas and pesto to the quinoa. Stir gently until well combined. Serve in a bowl.

NUTRITION - AMOUNT PER SERVING

Calories	356	Sugar	5g
Fat	10g	Protein	28g
Carbs	40g	Cholesterol	30mg
Fiber	7g	Sodium	361mg

REFER TO GRAPES ON PAGE 36 FOR QUANTITY AND NUTRITIONAL INFORMATION

Snacks

Tuna with Bell Pepper

 10 Minutes

 1 Serving

INGREDIENTS

- ½ can Tuna (drained)
- 1 tbsp Cream Cheese, Regular
- Sea Salt & Black Pepper (to taste)
- ½ Yellow Bell Pepper (sliced)

INSTRUCTIONS

1. Mix the tuna, cream cheese, salt and pepper together. Serve with the bell pepper and enjoy!

NUTRITION - AMOUNT PER SERVING

Calories	140	Sugar	1g
Fat	5g	Protein	18g
Carbs	6g	Cholesterol	43mg
Fiber	1g	Sodium	271mg

Pecans & Blueberries

 5 Minutes

 1 Serving

INGREDIENTS

- 1 cup Blueberries
- ¼ cup Pecans

INSTRUCTIONS

1. Serve the blueberries with pecans in a bowl and enjoy!

NUTRITION - AMOUNT PER SERVING

Calories	255	Sugar	16g
Fat	18g	Protein	3g
Carbs	25g	Cholesterol	0mg
Fiber	6g	Sodium	1mg

Cottage Cheese & Orange

 5 Minutes

 1 Serving

INGREDIENTS

- 1 Navel Orange (large, chopped)
- 1 cup Cottage Cheese

INSTRUCTIONS

1. Serve the chopped orange with the cottage cheese.

NUTRITION - AMOUNT PER SERVING

Calories	274	Sugar	18g
Fat	9g	Protein	25g
Carbs	25g	Cholesterol	36mg
Fiber	3g	Sodium	663mg

Bell Peppers with Hummus

 5 Minutes

 1 Serving

INGREDIENTS

- 1 Red Bell Pepper (medium, sliced)
- ¼ cup Hummus

INSTRUCTIONS

1. Plate the red bell pepper slices and hummus on a plate and enjoy.
2. Enjoy by dipping the bell peppers into the hummus!

NUTRITION - AMOUNT PER SERVING

Calories	177	Sugar	15g
Fat	11g	Protein	6g
Carbs	16g	Cholesterol	0mg
Fiber	6g	Sodium	267mg

Cottage Cheese with Blueberries

 5 Minutes

 1 Serving

INGREDIENTS

- ½ cup Cottage Cheese
- ¼ cup Blueberries (fresh or frozen)

INSTRUCTIONS

1. Add the cottage cheese and blueberries to a bowl to enjoy.

NUTRITION - AMOUNT PER SERVING

Calories	124	Sugar	6g
Fat	5g	Protein	12g
Carbs	9g	Cholesterol	18mg
Fiber	1g	Sodium	331mg

Peach Yogurt Parfait

 5 Minutes

 1 Serving

INGREDIENTS

- ½ cup Unsweetened Coconut Yogurt
- ½ cup Granola
- ½ Peach (pit removed, sliced)

INSTRUCTIONS

1. Layer the yogurt, granola, and peach in a jar or glass.

NUTRITION - AMOUNT PER SERVING

Calories	383	Sugar	19g
Fat	19g	Protein	10g
Carbs	46g	Cholesterol	0mg
Fiber	8g	Sodium	41mg

Tuna & Kale Chips

 10 Minutes

 1 Serving

INGREDIENTS

- 2 cups Kale Leaves (tough stems removed, torn into pieces)
- ½ can Tuna (drained)
- 2 tbsps Unsweetened Coconut Yogurt
- ⅛ tsp Sea Salt (to taste)

INSTRUCTIONS

1. Preheat oven to 350°F (176°C). Line a baking tray with parchment paper.
2. Place the kale in a single layer on the baking tray. Bake for about 10 to 15 minutes or until crispy.
3. While the kale is in the oven, mix the tuna, coconut yogurt, and salt in a bowl.
4. Serve the tuna mix with the kale chips and enjoy!

NUTRITION - AMOUNT PER SERVING

Calories	99	Sugar	1g
Fat	2g	Protein	17g
Carbs	3g	Cholesterol	30mg
Fiber	2g	Sodium	527mg

WEEK 3

7-Days Meal Plan

MONDAY

BREAKFAST
Apple Cinnamon Yogurt Bowl

LUNCH
Spinach Tuna Crepes, Pineapple

DINNER
Creamy Chicken Chickpea Pasta, Fresh Strawberries

SNACKS
Date, Chia & Tahini Energy Balls

TUESDAY

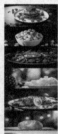

BREAKFAST
Cinnamon Oatmeal Pancakes, Macadamia Nuts & Walnuts

LUNCH
Pesto Chicken & Tomatoes with Quinoa, Pineapple

DINNER
Herb Crusted Haddock, Baked Potato

SNACKS
Chia Oats with Kiwi

WEDNESDAY

BREAKFAST
Tortilla Breakfast Wrap

LUNCH
One Pan Salmon, Zucchini & Bell Peppers, Orange

DINNER
Spicy Beef with Egg, Grapefruit

SNACKS
Apple Slices with Peanut Butter Yogurt

THURSDAY

BREAKFAST
Feta, Pepper & Olive Egg Muffins

LUNCH
Mediterranean Tuna Salad, Blueberries

DINNER
Braised Chicken with Chickpeas & Kale, Fresh Strawberries

SNACKS
Greek Yogurt & Peanut Butter Rice Cakes

FRIDAY

BREAKFAST
Cottage Cheese Pancakes, Almonds

LUNCH
Haddock, Broccoli & Quinoa, Banana

DINNER
Chicken, Kale & Avocado, Grapefruit

SNACKS
Frozen Yogurt Bites with Berries

SATURDAY

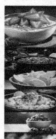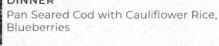

BREAKFAST
Plain Omelet with Cucumber

LUNCH
Roasted Chicken & Sweet Potato with Spinach, Banana

DINNER
Seared Cod & Lemon White Beans, Grapes

SNACKS
Yogurt with Banana, Nuts & Seeds

SUNDAY

BREAKFAST
Coconut Chia Seed Yogurt

LUNCH
Lemon Turkey Quinoa Skillet, Orange

DINNER
Pan Seared Cod with Cauliflower Rice, Blueberries

SNACKS
Strawberries & Cottage Cheese

Shopping List

FRUITS

1 ½ Apples
½ Avocado
3 ½ Bananas
2 cups Blueberries
2 Grapefruit
1 cup Grapes
½ Kiwi
¾ Lemon
½ tbsps Lemon Juice
2 Navel Oranges
3 cups Pineapple
2 ⅓ tsps Pomegranate Seeds
1 ⅙ tbsps Raspberries
2 ¾ cups Strawberries

SEEDS, NUTS & SPICES

½ cup Almonds
2 ⅔ tbsps Cashews
⅓ cup Chia Seeds
2 tsps Cinnamon
⅛ tsp Dried Thyme
⅔ tsp Garlic Powder
2 tbsps Macadamia Nuts
⅓ tsp Onion Powder
½ tsp Oregano
¼ tsp Paprika
2 ⅔ tbsps Pecans
2 ²⁄₄ tbsps Pumpkin Seeds
⅛ tsp Red Pepper Flakes
Sea Salt & Black Pepper
2 tbsps Walnuts

VEGETABLES

1 ¼ cups Arugula
5 ⅔ cups Baby Spinach
1 ¼ cups Cherry Tomatoes
3 Cremini Mushrooms
⅔ Cucumber
1 ¾ tbsps Fresh Dill
3 ⅛ Garlic
¾ tsp Ginger
⅛ Green Bell Pepper
2 stalks Green Onion
4 cups Kale Leaves
3 ½ tbsps Parsley
⅔ Red Bell Pepper
2 tbsps Red Onion
¼ cup Shallots
½ Sweet Potato
1 tsp Thyme
3 White Button Mushrooms
1 Russet Potato
½ Zucchini

PANTRY STAPLES

¼ cup All Natural Peanut Butter
2 Plain Rice Cakes
1 tbsp Bread Crumbs
1 cup Cannellini Beans
½ cup Chicken Broth
50 grams Chickpea Pasta
½ cup Chickpeas
⅔ cup Quinoa
1 ⅓ tbsps Tomato Paste
1 can Tuna
⅓ cup Vegetable Broth
½ cup White Navy Beans

BAKING

¼ tsp Baking Powder
1 cup Oats
2 ⅔ Pitted Dates

BREAD, FISH, MEAT & CHEESE

284 grams Chicken Breast
226 grams Chicken Thighs
2 Cod Fillets
113 grams Extra Lean Ground Beef
113 grams Extra Lean Ground Turkey
2 tbsps Feta Cheese
2 Haddock Fillets
142 grams Salmon Fillet
1 Whole Wheat Tortilla

CONDIMENTS & OILS

1 ½ tbsps Coconut Oil
½ tsp Dijon Mustard
½ cup Extra Virgin Olive Oil
1 ¼ tsps Pesto
5 ⅓ tbsps Pitted Calamata Olives
2 tsps Tahini
1 ½ tsps Tamari

FRIDGE

1 ⅛ cups Cottage Cheese
11 Eggs
3 cups Plain Greek Yogurt
¾ cup Unsweetened Almond Milk
1 ⅛ cups Unsweetened Coconut Yogurt

Apple Cinnamon Yogurt Bowl

 10 Minutes

 1 Serving

INGREDIENTS

- ½ tsp Coconut Oil
- ½ Apple (large, peeled and cut into small cubes)
- ¼ tsp Cinnamon
- ½ cup Plain Greek Yogurt
- 2 ⅔ tbsps Pecans (chopped)

INSTRUCTIONS

1. Over medium-low heat, melt the coconut oil in a small saucepan.
2. Once melted, add the apple and cinnamon. Stirring often, sauté for 8 to 10 minutes until soft.
3. Pour the yogurt into a bowl and top with the cooked apples and chopped pecans.

NUTRITION - AMOUNT PER SERVING

Calories	274	Sugar	13g
Fat	17g	Protein	13g
Carbs	21g	Cholesterol	17mg
Fiber	4g	Sodium	71mg

Cinnamon Oatmeal Pancakes

 25 Minutes

 1 Serving

INGREDIENTS

- ¼ cup Oats (rolled)
- ¼ tsp Baking Powder
- ⅔ tsp Cinnamon
- 1 Egg
- ⅓ cup Unsweetened Almond Milk
- 1 ¼ tsps Coconut Oil (divided)
- 2 ⅓ tsps Pomegranate Seeds
- 1 ¹⁄₁₆ tbsps Raspberries
- 2 ⅓ tsps Pumpkin Seeds

INSTRUCTIONS

1. Process the rolled oats in a food processor until a flour-like consistency is created. Add baking powder and cinnamon to the oats and pulse to combine.
2. Add the egg, almond milk, and half of the coconut oil to the oat mixture and continue to process until well combined.
3. Warm the remaining oil in a large non-stick pan or skillet over medium heat. Once the coconut oil has melted, spoon the batter into the skillet to form one small pancake.
4. As soon as small holes begin to appear on the surface of the pancake, flip it over. Cook each side for 3 to 4 minutes. Repeat until the batter is finished.
5. Top the pancakes with pomegranate seeds, raspberries, and pumpkin seeds.

NUTRITION - AMOUNT PER SERVING

Calories	258	Sugar	2g
Fat	16g	Protein	11g
Carbs	19g	Cholesterol	186mg
Fiber	4g	Sodium	248mg

Macadamia Nuts & Walnuts

 5 Minutes

 1 Serving

INGREDIENTS

- 2 tbsps Macadamia Nuts
- 2 tbsps Walnuts

INSTRUCTIONS

1. In a small bowl combine the macadamia nuts and walnuts.

NUTRITION - AMOUNT PER SERVING

Calories	218	Sugar	1g
Fat	22g	Protein	4g
Carbs	4g	Cholesterol	0mg
Fiber	2g	Sodium	1mg

Tortilla Breakfast Wrap

 15 Minutes

 1 Serving

INGREDIENTS

- ½ tsp Extra Virgin Olive Oil
- 3 Cremini Mushrooms (sliced)
- 1 ½ cups Baby Spinach
- 2 Eggs
- Sea Salt & Black Pepper (to taste)
- 1 Whole Wheat Tortilla (medium size)

INSTRUCTIONS

1. Spoon the oil into a pan and warm it over medium-low heat.
2. Add the sliced mushrooms and sauté until water is released and the mushrooms have browned, about 5 minutes. Season with salt and pepper. Remove and set aside.
3. Add the spinach to the skillet and sauté over medium-low heat until just wilted. Set aside with the mushrooms.
4. In a small bowl whisk the eggs. Add the whisked eggs and cook over medium-low heat until cooked to your liking. Season with salt and pepper.
5. Lay the tortilla on a flat surface and layer with eggs, mushrooms, and spinach. Roll or fold the tortilla together to enjoy!

NUTRITION - AMOUNT PER SERVING

Calories	292	Sugar	3g
Fat	14g	Protein	20g
Carbs	23g	Cholesterol	372mg
Fiber	6g	Sodium	433mg

Feta, Pepper & Olive Egg Muffins

 30 Minutes

 1 Serving

INGREDIENTS

- 2 Eggs
- ¼ tsp Oregano
- ⅛ tsp Garlic Powder
- Sea Salt & Black Pepper (to taste)
- ⅛ Green Bell Pepper (medium, diced)
- ⅛ Red Bell Pepper (medium, diced)
- 1 tbsp Pitted Kalamata Olives (chopped)
- 2 tbsps Feta Cheese (crumbled)

INSTRUCTIONS

1. Preheat oven to 400°F (205°C). Grease a muffin tray lightly or use a silicone muffin tray.

2. In a bowl, whisk the eggs. Stir in the oregano, garlic powder, salt, and pepper. Add the bell peppers, olives, and feta. Gently stir.

3. Divide the egg mixture in the muffin tray, about 3/4 of the way full. Bake for 15 to 18 minutes or until set and browned on the sides. Let them cool for about 5 minutes.

NUTRITION - AMOUNT PER SERVING

Calories	211	Sugar	1g
Fat	15g	Protein	16g
Carbs	4g	Cholesterol	389mg
Fiber	1g	Sodium	419mg

Cottage Cheese Pancakes

 15 Minutes

 1 Serving

INGREDIENTS

- 3 tbsps Cottage Cheese
- 1 Egg (large)
- ¼ cup Oats (rolled or quick)
- 1 tsp Extra Virgin Olive Oil (divided)

INSTRUCTIONS

1. Add the cottage cheese, eggs, and oats to a blender. Blend until smooth.
2. Heat a little of the oil over medium-low heat setting in a non-stick pan. Add 1/4 cup of batter, cooking for about 3 to 4 minutes per side until golden brown. Repeat with the remaining batter and oil.
3. Plate and enjoy!

NUTRITION - AMOUNT PER SERVING

Calories	227	Sugar	1g
Fat	12g	Protein	13g
Carbs	15g	Cholesterol	193mg
Fiber	2g	Sodium	196mg

REFER TO ALMONDS ON PAGE 23 FOR QUANTITY AND NUTRITIONAL INFORMATION

Plain Omelet with Cucumbers

 10 Minutes

 1 Serving

INGREDIENTS

- 3 Eggs
- Sea Salt & Black Pepper (to taste)
- 1 tsp Extra Virgin Olive Oil
- ½ Cucumber (medium, sliced)

INSTRUCTIONS

1. In a small bowl whisk eggs. Season with sea salt and black pepper.
2. In a small non-stick skillet, warm the olive oil.
3. Pour the whisked eggs into the non-stick skillet and cook over a medium heat until almost set. Fold in half, cook for another minute, and transfer the omelet to a plate.
4. Serve with cucumber slices!

NUTRITION - AMOUNT PER SERVING

Calories	277	Sugar	3g
Fat	19g	Protein	20g
Carbs	7g	Cholesterol	558mg
Fiber	1g	Sodium	216mg

Coconut Chia Seed Yogurt

 30 Minutes

 1 Serving

INGREDIENTS

- 1 cup Unsweetened Coconut Yogurt
- ¼ cup Chia Seeds
- 1 tsp Cinnamon
- ¼ cup Strawberries (chopped)

INSTRUCTIONS

1. Mix the yogurt, chia seeds, and cinnamon in a small bowl. Combine well and refrigerate for at least 30 minutes or overnight.
2. Top with strawberries and enjoy!

NUTRITION - AMOUNT PER SERVING

Calories	355	Sugar	3g
Fat	22g	Protein	9g
Carbs	37g	Cholesterol	0mg
Fiber	21g	Sodium	57mg

Spinach Tuna Crepes

 35 Minutes

 1 Serving

INGREDIENTS

- ½ cup Baby Spinach
- 1 tbsp Parsley
- ½ cup unsweetened Almond Milk
- 1 Egg
- ⅓ cup Whole Wheat Flour Sea Salt & Black Pepper (to taste)
- 1 ½ tsps Extra Virgin Olive Oil
- ½ can Tuna (drained and flaked)
- ⅓ cup Cherry Tomatoes (halved)
- ¾ tsp Fresh Dill (chopped)

INSTRUCTIONS

1. Blend the spinach, parsley, almond milk, and eggs until smooth. Slowly add the flour until thoroughly combined. Season with salt and pepper to taste.
2. Brush a medium non-stick skillet with olive oil over a medium heat. When the olive oil is hot, pour 1/4 cup of the crepe batter into the skillet and carefully swirl to spread it into a thin layer. Cook for about 1 minute on each side. Repeat with the remaining batter.
3. Plate the crepes. Spoon tuna in the middle along with cherry tomatoes. Sprinkle dill on top. Roll or fold the crepes to enjoy.

NUTRITION - AMOUNT PER SERVING

Calories	377	Sugar	2g
Fat	15g	Protein	29g
Carbs	33g	Cholesterol	216mg
Fiber	7g	Sodium	372mg

REFER TO PINEAPPLE ON PAGE 84 FOR QUANTITY AND NUTRITIONAL INFORMATION

Pesto Chicken & Tomatoes with Quinoa

 20 Minutes

 1 Serving

INGREDIENTS

- ¼ cup Quinoa (dry)
- 113 grams Chicken Thighs (boneless, skinless)
- ¼ cup Cherry Tomatoes (halved)
- 1 ¼ tsps Pesto
- 1 cup Baby Spinach

INSTRUCTIONS

1. Preheat oven to 375°F (190°C). Line a baking tray with parchment paper.
2. Following the package directions, cook the quinoa.
3. Toss the chicken thighs and cherry tomatoes with the pesto until well coated. Add the chicken and tomatoes to the baking tray. Bake for 15 to 20 minutes until the chicken is cooked. Add the spinach to the chicken and tomatoes and cook for a further 1 - 2 minutes.
4. Plate the quinoa in a bowl and top with the chicken and vegetables. For extra flavor, spoon residual sauce from the baking tray on top.

NUTRITION - AMOUNT PER SERVING

Calories	335	Sugar	2g
Fat	10g	Protein	30g
Carbs	30g	Cholesterol	107mg
Fiber	4g	Sodium	175mg

REFER TO PINEAPPLE ON PAGE 84 FOR QUANTITY AND NUTRITIONAL INFORMATION

One Pan Salmon, Zucchini & Bell Peppers

 35 Minutes

 1 Serving

INGREDIENTS

- ½ Red Bell Pepper (medium, sliced)
- ½ Zucchini (medium, sliced into strips)
- ½ tsp Extra Virgin Olive Oil
- Sea Salt & Black Pepper (to taste)
- 142 grams Salmon Fillet
- 1 ½ tsps Fresh Dill
- ¼ Lemon (sliced into wedges, to serve)

INSTRUCTIONS

1. Preheat oven to 400°F (204°C). Line a baking tray with parchment paper.
2. Scatter the bell peppers and zucchini on the parchment paper and toss with oil. Season with salt and pepper. Bake in the oven for about 15 minutes. Remove from oven and set the vegetables aside.
3. After seasoning the salmon with sea salt and black pepper, place it on the used baking tray. Bake for 15 to 20 minutes or until cooked through.
4. Transfer the salmon to a serving dish. Top with the bell peppers, zucchini and fresh dill with lemon on the side.

NUTRITION - AMOUNT PER SERVING

Calories	240	Sugar	5g
Fat	9g	Protein	33g
Carbs	7g	Cholesterol	72mg
Fiber	2g	Sodium	121mg

REFER TO ORANGE ON PAGE 32 FOR QUANTITY AND NUTRITIONAL INFORMATION

Mediterranean Tuna Salad

 10 Minutes

 1 Serving

INGREDIENTS

- ½ can Tuna (drained)
- ½ cup Cherry Tomatoes (halved)
- 2 tbsps Pitted Kalamata Olives (halved)
- 2 tbsps Red Onion (sliced)
- 1 cup Cannellini Beans (drained and rinsed)
- 1 tbsp Extra Virgin Olive Oil
- 1 ½ tsps Lemon Juice
- 1 ½ tbsps Parsley (finely chopped)
- Sea Salt & Black Pepper (to taste)

INSTRUCTIONS

1. Mix the tuna, tomatoes, olives, red onion, beans, olive oil, and parsley in a medium-sized bowl. Mix in the lemon juice, sea salt, and black pepper and toss to combine.
2. Serve in a bowl and enjoy!

NUTRITION - AMOUNT PER SERVING

Calories	448	Sugar	5g
Fat	19g	Protein	26g
Carbs	44g	Cholesterol	30mg
Fiber	12g	Sodium	1053mg

REFER TO BLUEBERRIES ON PAGE 46 FOR QUANTITY AND NUTRITIONAL INFORMATION

Haddock, Broccoli & Quinoa

 25 Minutes

 1 Serving

INGREDIENTS

- ¼ cup Quinoa (uncooked)
- 1 Haddock Fillet
- 1 cup Frozen Broccoli
- 1 tbsp Coconut Oil
- ¼ tsp Onion Powder
- ¼ tsp Paprika
- ¼ tsp Sea Salt

INSTRUCTIONS

1. Preheat oven to 450°F (232°C). Line a baking sheet with parchment paper.
2. Cook the quinoa according to package directions.
3. Place the haddock and broccoli on the parchment paper. Use a whisk to mix the onion powder, paprika, coconut oil, and sea salt in a small bowl. Brush the mixture onto the haddock and broccoli.
4. Bake the haddock and broccoli for 20 minutes until the fish is cooked and the broccoli has softened. Serve with the quinoa and enjoy!

NUTRITION - AMOUNT PER SERVING

Calories	455	Sugar	2g
Fat	17g	Protein	40g
Carbs	34g	Cholesterol	104mg
Fiber	6g	Sodium	1034mg

REFER TO BANANA ON PAGE 78 FOR QUANTITY AND NUTRITIONAL INFORMATION

Roasted Chicken & Sweet Potato with Spinach

 25 Minutes

 1 Serving

INGREDIENTS

- ½ Sweet Potato (medium, cut into cubes)
- 142 grams Chicken Breast (skinless, boneless)
- ½ tsp Thyme (fresh)
- ½ tsp Garlic Powder
- Sea Salt & Black Pepper (to taste)
- 1 ½ cups Baby Spinach

INSTRUCTIONS

1. Preheat oven to 400°F (204°C). Line a baking sheet with parchment paper.
2. Place the sweet potatoes and chicken breast on the baking sheet. Season all with thyme, garlic powder, salt, and pepper. Bake for 18 to 20 minutes until the chicken is thoroughly cooked and the sweet potatoes are golden and slightly crispy.
3. Plate with the spinach on the side.

NUTRITION - AMOUNT PER SERVING

Calories	241	Sugar	3g
Fat	4g	Protein	34g
Carbs	16g	Cholesterol	103 mg
Fiber	3g	Sodium	136 mg

REFER TO BANANA ON PAGE 78 FOR QUANTITY AND NUTRITIONAL INFORMATION

Lemon Turkey Quinoa Skillet

 30 Minutes

 1 Serving

INGREDIENTS

- 1 ⅛ tsps Extra Virgin Olive Oil
- ½ Garlic (cloves, minced)
- 113 grams Extra Lean Ground Turkey
- ¼ tsp Oregano (dried)
- ¹⁄₁₆ tsp Sea Salt
- 1 tbsp Pitted Calamata Olives(chopped)
- ½ cup Baby Spinach (chopped)
- 3 tbsps Quinoa (dry, uncooked)
- ⅓ cup Vegetable Broth
- ¼ Lemon (zested and juiced)

INSTRUCTIONS

1. In a large skillet with a lid, heat the olive oil over a medium-high heat setting.
2. Add the minced garlic to the skillet and cook it for about 1 minute, or until it becomes fragrant. Add the turkey, oregano, and salt and cook for about 5 to 7 minutes until the turkey is cooked, breaking it up as it cooks.
3. Add the calamata olives and baby spinach to the skillet and mix well with the turkey until the spinach is wilted.
4. Pour the quinoa into the skillet and stir it to combine with the vegetables and turkey. Next, pour in the vegetable broth. Bring the mixture to a gentle boil.
5. Place a lid over the skillet and lower the heat to medium-low. Allow the skillet to simmer for 10 to 12 minutes, or until all the liquid has been absorbed and the quinoa is tender.
6. Mix in the lemon zest and juice. Taste and add more salt if necessary. Plate and enjoy!

NUTRITION - AMOUNT PER SERVING

Calories	355	Sugar	1g
Fat	18g	Protein	27g
Carbs	24g	Cholesterol	84 mg
Fiber	3g	Sodium	547 mg

REFER TO ORANGE ON PAGE 32 FOR QUANTITY AND NUTRITIONAL INFORMATION

Dinners

Creamy Chicken Chickpea Pasta

 25 Minutes  1 Serving

INGREDIENTS

- 50 grams Chickpea Pasta (dry)
- 1 tsp Extra Virgin Olive Oil
- 1 ⅓ tbsps Shallots (chopped)
- 1 ⅓ tbsps Tomato Paste
- ⅔ Garlic (clove, thinly sliced)
- 113 grams Chicken Thighs (boneless, skinless,
- chopped into bite-size pieces)
- Sea Salt & Black Pepper (to taste)
- 2 ⅔ tbsps Cashews
- ⅓ cup Water (reserved from cooking pasta, divided)
- ⅔ cup Baby Spinach

INSTRUCTIONS

1. Cook the pasta according to package directions. Reserve some pasta water for later.
2. Add the oil to a large pot and warm over medium-low heat. As soon as the oil is hot, add the shallots and sauté for 2 minutes, stirring often, until softened. Add the tomato paste, stirring often as it cooks, until deep red, about 5 minutes.
3. Next, toss in the sliced garlic and cook for another minute. Then add the chopped chicken and season with salt and pepper. Continue to cook for another 11 to 13 minutes until the chicken is cooked, stirring occasionally.
4. Combine the cashews and 3/4 of the reserved water in a blender. Blend until smooth and creamy.
5. Add the spinach to the pot and sauté until just wilted. Add pasta and the remaining water to the pot and turn the heat to low. Add the cashew cream and toss until coated and warmed through.

NUTRITION - AMOUNT PER SERVING

Calories	501	Sugar	9g
Fat	23g	Protein	39g
Carbs	42g	Cholesterol	107mg
Fiber	9g	Sodium	193mg

REFER TO STRAWBERRIES ON PAGE 48 FOR QUANTITY AND NUTRITIONAL INFORMATION

Herb Crusted Haddock

 20 Minutes

 **1 Serving**

INGREDIENTS

- 1 tbsp Parsley (chopped)
- 1 tbsp Fresh Dill (chopped)
- 1 tbsp Bread Crumbs
- ½ Garlic (clove, minced)
- ¼ Lemon (medium, juiced, zested)
- Sea Salt & Black Pepper (to taste)
- 1 Haddock Fillet

INSTRUCTIONS

1. Preheat oven to 400°F (204°C). Line a baking sheet with parchment paper.
2. Mix parsley, dill, bread crumbs, garlic, lemon juice, and lemon zest in a bowl. Season the mixture with salt and pepper.
3. Place the haddock fillets on the baking sheet and spoon the herb mixture on top of the haddock. Gently press it down.
4. Bake the haddock for 10 to 12 minutes or until cooked through.
5. Use the residual herb juices over the baked potato (next recipe).

NUTRITION - AMOUNT PER SERVING

Calories	176	Sugar	1g
Fat	1g	Protein	33g
Carbs	6g	Cholesterol	104mg
Fiber	1g	Sodium	463mg

Baked Potato

 45 Minutes  1 Serving

INGREDIENTS

- 1 Russet Potato (large)
- ¼ tsp Extra Virgin Olive Oil (optional)
- 1⁄16 tsp Sea Salt (optional)

INSTRUCTIONS

1. Preheat oven to 400°F (204°C). Scrub the potato and pierce it multiple times with a sharp knife or fork.
2. Lightly coat the potato in oil and season with salt (optional). Place the potato onto a baking tray and bake for approximately 45 minutes until cooked and tender.
3. To serve, use a sharp knife to cut down the center of the potato, then carefully squeeze the ends together to open.

NUTRITION - AMOUNT PER SERVING

Calories	174
Fat	1g
Carbs	37g
Fiber	4g
Sugar	29
Protein	5g
Cholesterol	0mg
Sodium	172mg

Grapefruit

5 Minutes   1 Serving

INGREDIENTS

- 1 Grapefruit

INSTRUCTIONS

1. Cut a grapefruit in half and place in a bowl. Use a sharp knife to cut around the circumference.
2. Use a spoon to scoop out individual sections.

NUTRITION - AMOUNT PER SERVING

Calories	82
Fat	0g
Carbs	21g
Fiber	3g
Sugar	18g
Protein	2g
Cholesterol	0mg
Sodium	0mg

Spicy Beef with Egg

 25 Minutes

 1 Serving

INGREDIENTS

- 1 ½ tsps Tamari
- 1 Garlic (large clove, minced)
- ⅛ tsp Red Pepper Flakes
- ½ stalk Green Onion (chopped, divided)
- 113 grams Extra Lean Ground Beef
- 1½ tbsps Extra Virgin Olive Oil (divided)
- 1 ½ cups Cauliflower Rice
- 1 Egg
- ⅛ Cucumber (thinly sliced, optional)

INSTRUCTIONS

1. Add the tamari, garlic, red pepper flakes, and half of the green onion to a small bowl and stir to combine.
2. Heat a pan over a medium heat. Add the beef to the hot pan, breaking it up as it cooks. Drain any excess drippings from the pan once it is cooked through and no longer pink.
3. Add the tamari sauce mix to the pan and cook for 2 to 3 more minutes until the meat has absorbed the sauce. Remove from the heat and set aside.
4. Warm ⅔ of the olive oil in another small non-stick pan over a medium heat. Pour in the cauliflower rice and cook for 3 to 5 minutes. When cooked, plate the cauliflower rice.
5. Spoon the remaining olive oil into the same pan and cook the egg to your preference.
6. Add the beef to the cauliflower rice and top with the egg, sliced cucumber, and the remaining green onion.

NUTRITION - AMOUNT PER SERVING

Calories	512	Sugar	36g
Fat	4g	Protein	33g
Carbs	10g	Cholesterol	259mg
Fiber	4g	Sodium	689 mg

Braised Chicken with Chickpeas & Kale

 1 Hour

 1 Serving

INGREDIENTS

- 142 grams Chicken Breast (bone-in, skin-on)
- Sea Salt & Black Pepper (to taste)
- 2 tsps Extra Virgin Olive Oil
- 2 ⅔ Shallots (chopped)
- ⅓ cup Chicken Broth
- ½ tsp Dijon Mustard
- 1½ tsps. Lemon Juice
- 2 cups Kale Leaves (chopped)
- ½ cup Chickpeas (cooked)

INSTRUCTIONS

1. With a paper towel pat the chicken dry and season with salt and pepper.
2. Over a medium heat setting, heat the olive oil in a deep pan that has a lid.
3. Once hot, place the chicken skin side down, uncovered, and cook until golden brown, about 5 minutes.
4. Remove and set aside.
5. Turn the heat down to medium-low and add the shallots. Cook until softened, about 3 minutes. Add the chicken broth, Dijon, and lemon juice and bring to a simmer.
6. Add the kale and chickpeas and stir to combine. Place the chicken in the pot, skin side up. Use the lid to cover the pan. Reduce the heat again. Simmer for 30 - 35 minutes until the chicken is cooked through.
7. Plate the chicken, kale, and chickpeas with any remaining liquid and enjoy.

NUTRITION - AMOUNT PER SERVING

Calories	427	Sugar	7g
Fat	16g	Protein	41g
Carbs	30g	Cholesterol	105mg
Fiber	9g	Sodium	430mg

REFER TO STRAWBERRIES ON PAGE 48 FOR QUANTITY AND NUTRITIONAL INFORMATION

Chicken, Kale & Avocado

 20 Minutes   **1 Serving**

INGREDIENTS

- 1 ½ tsps Extra Virgin Olive Oil
- 3 White Button Mushrooms (sliced)
- 2 cups Kale Leaves (chopped)
- 1/16 tsp Sea Salt (divided)
- 113 grams Extra Lean Ground Chicken
- 1/8 tsp Dried Thyme
- 1/8 tsp Onion Powder
- 1/16 tsp Oregano
- 1/16 tsp Garlic Powder
- ½ Avocado (sliced)

INSTRUCTIONS

1. In a large skillet heat the oil over a medium heat setting. Add the sliced mushrooms and cook for 8 to 10 minutes, until cooked through. Add the kale leaves and stir, cooking until just wilted. Season with half of the sea salt. Remove from the skillet and set aside for later.

2. In the same skillet, add the chicken, thyme, onion powder, oregano, garlic, and the remaining sea salt over a medium heat setting. Cook for 10 to 12 minutes until thoroughly cooked. During the last minute, add the cooked mushroom mix to reheat.

3. Plate and top with sliced avocado.

NUTRITION - AMOUNT PER SERVING

Calories	411	Sugar	29
Fat	31g	Protein	25g
Carbs	13g	Cholesterol	98mg
Fiber	9g	Sodium	248mg

REFER TO GRAPEFRUIT ON PAGE 119 FOR QUANTITY AND NUTRITIONAL INFORMATION

Seared Cod & Lemon White Beans

 20 Minutes

 1 Serving

INGREDIENTS

- 1 Cod Fillet
- ¹⁄₁₆ tsp Sea Salt
- 1 ½ tbsps Extra Virgin Olive Oil
- ½ Garlic (cloves, minced)
- ½ tsp Thyme (fresh, minced)
- 3 tbsps Cherry Tomatoes (halved)
- 3 tbsps Chicken Broth
- ½ cup White Navy Beans
- 1 ¼ cups Arugula
- 1 ½ tsps Lemon Juice
- 1 ⅓ tbsps Pitted Kalamata Olives

INSTRUCTIONS

1. Season the cod with sea salt and preheat a skillet over medium heat. Add the oil to the skillet and, once warm, add the cod. Cook for 4 minutes per side, until cooked through. Remove the cod from the skillet and set aside for later.

2. In the same skillet, reduce the heat to medium-low and add the garlic. Sauté the garlic for 1 minute, then add the thyme and cherry tomatoes. Cook for 2 to 3 minutes. Pour in the chicken broth and white beans and simmer for 3 to 5 minutes. Add the arugula, lemon juice and olives and stir until the arugula is wilted.

3. Plate the bean and vegetable mix and top with the cod.

NUTRITION - AMOUNT PER SERVING

Calories	527	Sugar	2g
Fat	24g	Protein	50g
Carbs	28g	Cholesterol	100mg
Fiber	11g	Sodium	537mg

REFER TO GRAPES ON PAGE 36 FOR QUANTITY AND NUTRITIONAL INFORMATION

Pan Seared Cod with Cauliflower Rice

 20 Minutes

 1 Serving

INGREDIENTS

- 1 Cod Fillet
- ¾ tsp Ginger (fresh, minced)
- 1 tbsp Extra Virgin Olive Oil (divided)
- 1 ½ cups Cauliflower Rice
- ¾ tsp Lime Juice
- 1 ½ stalks Green Onion (green and white parts divided, sliced)
- 1/8 tsp Sea Salt

INSTRUCTIONS

1. Marinate the cod, ginger, and half of the oil in a bowl. While marinating, prepare the cauliflower rice.

2. In a skillet over medium heat. Add the remaining oil and the cauliflower rice and sauté for 5 to 7 minutes. Add the lime juice to the cauliflower rice and stir to combine. Remove the cauliflower rice and set aside for later.

3. Add the cod, skin side down, and marinade to the same skillet over medium-high heat.

4. Cook the cod for 2 to 3 minutes until the skin is crisp and brown.

5. Flip the cod over and cook and continue cooking for an additional 5 minutes after adding the sliced white parts of the green onion.

6. To reheat the cauliflower rice, add it to the skillet next to the cod in the last minute of cooking.

7. Plate the cauliflower rice and top with the cod. Garnish the cod with the sliced green part of the onion. Sprinkle with the salt and enjoy!

NUTRITION - AMOUNT PER SERVING

Calories	361	Sugar	44g
Fat	15g	Protein	99mg
Carbs	8g	Cholesterol	3g
Fiber	4g	Sodium	461mg

REFER TO BLUEBERRIES ON PAGE 46 FOR QUANTITY AND NUTRITIONAL INFORMATION

Snacks

Date, Chia & Tahini Energy Balls

 35 Minutes

 1 Serving

INGREDIENTS

- 2 ⅔ tbsps Pitted Dates
- 2 tsps Tahini
- 2 tsps Chia Seeds
- 2 tsps Unsweetened Shredded Coconut

INSTRUCTIONS

1. In a blender add the dates, tahini, and chia seeds. Blend until smooth paste forms.
2. Use an ice cream scoop to scoop out the paste. Roll the paste in your hands to create a ball. Continue until you have used up all of the paste.
3. Coat each ball in shredded coconut. Chill in the fridge for about 30 minutes and enjoy!

NUTRITION - AMOUNT PER SERVING

Calories	189	Sugar	16g
Fat	10g	Protein	4g
Carbs	25g	Cholesterol	0mg
Fiber	6g	Sodium	14mg

Chia Oats with Kiwi

 10 Minutes

 1 Serving

INGREDIENTS

- ½ cup Water
- ½ cup Oats (rolled)
- 1 tbsp Chia Seeds
- ½ Kiwi (chopped)

INSTRUCTIONS

1. In a small saucepan, bring the water to a boil and add the oats and chia seeds. Turn down the heat and allow to simmer for 4 to 5 minutes until cooked, stirring regularly.
2. Plate in a bowl and top with kiwi.

NUTRITION - AMOUNT PER SERVING

Calories	231	Sugar	4g
Fat	6g	Protein	8g
Carbs	37g	Cholesterol	0mg
Fiber	9g	Sodium	8mg

Apple Slices with Peanut Butter Yogurt

 5 Minutes

 1 Serving

INGREDIENTS

- ¾ cup Plain Greek Yogurt
- 2 tbsps All Natural Peanut Butter
- 1 Apple (cored and sliced)

INSTRUCTIONS

1. In a bowl, combine the yogurt with the peanut butter and mix well.
2. Serve with the apple slices for dipping.

NUTRITION - AMOUNT PER SERVING

Calories	423	Sugar	27g
Fat	21g	Protein	24g
Carbs	41g	Cholesterol	25mg
Fiber	6g	Sodium	112mg

Greek Yogurt & Peanut Butter Rice Cakes

 5 Minutes

 1 Serving

INGREDIENTS

- ¾ cup Plain Greek Yogurt
- 2 tbsps All Natural Peanut Butter
- 2 Plain Rice Cake
- ½ Banana (sliced)

INSTRUCTIONS

1. In a small bowl, combine the yogurt and peanut butter.
2. Divide the mix between the rice cakes. Top with sliced banana.

NUTRITION - AMOUNT PER SERVING

Calories	451	Sugar	21g
Fat	15g	Protein	26g
Carbs	44g	Cholesterol	25mg
Fiber	4g	Sodium	116mg

Frozen Yogurt Bites with Berries

 3 Hours

 1 Serving

INGREDIENTS

- 2 tbsps Unsweetened Coconut Yogurt
- 1 tbsp Frozen Blueberries (chopped)
- 1 tbsp Frozen Strawberries (chopped)

INSTRUCTIONS

1. Mix all the ingredients in a bowl until thoroughly combined. Spoon the yogurt mixture into an ice cube tray, tapping the tray on the counter to remove any air bubbles.
2. Place the tray in the freezer and let it freeze for 2 to 3 hours until solid.

NUTRITION - AMOUNT PER SERVING

Calories	24	Sugar	2g
Fat	1g	Protein	0g
Carbs	4g	Cholesterol	0mg
Fiber	1g	Sodium	7mg

Yogurt with Banana, Nuts & Seeds

 5 Minutes

 1 Serving

INGREDIENTS

- 1 cup Plain Greek Yogurt
- 1 Banana (sliced)
- ¼ cup Almonds
- 2 tbsps Pumpkin Seeds

INSTRUCTIONS

1. Add the yogurt, banana, almonds, and seeds to a bowl and enjoy!

NUTRITION - AMOUNT PER SERVING

Calories	583	Sugar	22g
Fat	31g	Protein	36g
Carbs	48g	Cholesterol	34mg
Fiber	9g	Sodium	143mg

Strawberries & Cottage Cheese

 5 Minutes

 1 Serving

INGREDIENTS

- 1 cup Cottage Cheese
- ½ cup Strawberries (sliced)

INSTRUCTIONS

1. Spoon the cottage cheese into a bowl.
2. Top with fresh sliced strawberries.

NUTRITION - AMOUNT PER SERVING

Calories	229	Sugar	9g
Fat	9g	Protein	24g
Carbs	13g	Cholesterol	36mg
Fiber	1g	Sodium	662mg

WEEK 4

7-Days Meal Plan

MONDAY

BREAKFAST
Quinoa & Kale Egg Muffins

LUNCH
One Pan Salmon & Fennel with Lime, Pineapple

DINNER
Zucchini & Ground Beef Skillet, Apple

SNACKS
Cherries & Greek Yogurt

TUESDAY

BREAKFAST
Almond Pancakes

LUNCH
One Pan Basil Chicken

DINNER
Shrimp Asparagus Pesto Pasta, Blueberries

SNACKS
Avocado Rice Cakes

WEDNESDAY

BREAKFAST
Coconut Hemp Seed Breakfast Pudding

LUNCH
Lemon Dill Baked Salmon, Peach

DINNER
Nicoise Salad, Cherries

SNACKS
Creamy Mango Pudding

THURSDAY

BREAKFAST
Pesto Eggs & Toast

LUNCH
Turkey Pesto Wrap

DINNER
Turkey Burger, Blueberries

SNACKS
Lemon Dill Yogurt Dip & Peppers

FRIDAY

BREAKFAST
Cottage Cheese with Cherries & Pumpkin Seeds

LUNCH
Chicken Avocado Wrap, Pineapple

DINNER
One Pan Chicken Thighs with Asparagus

SNACKS
Strawberries & Almonds

SATURDAY

BREAKFAST
Omelet & Fruits

LUNCH
Lemon Cilantro Cod with Peppers, Banana

DINNER
Lentil Stuffed Grilled Peppers, Cherries

SNACKS
Radish & Cucumber Rice Cakes

SUNDAY

BREAKFAST
Eggs & Toast

LUNCH
One Pan Halibut & Green Beans, Peach

DINNER
Beef Burrito Bowl with Cauliflower Rice, Apple

SNACKS
Greek Yogurt with Almonds & Pear

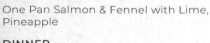

Shopping List

FRUITS

2 Apples
2 Avocados
1 Banana
2 cups Blueberries
2 ¾ cups Cherries
1 ⅓ Lemon
2 tbsps Lemon Juice
1 ¼ Limes
1 ½ tsps Lime Juice
½ cup Mixed Berries
2 Peaches
1 Pear
3 cups Pineapple
¼ cup Raspberries
1 cup Strawberries

SEEDS, NUTS & SPICES

½ cup Almonds
   Sea Salt & Black Pepper
1/16 tsp Cayenne Pepper
1 ½ tbsps Chia Seeds
⅛ tsp Cinnamon
¾ tsp Coriander
1 1/16 tsps Cumin
⅛ tsp Fennel Seeds
1 ½ tbsps Ground Flax
   Seeds
¼ cup Hemp Seeds
1/16 tsp Onion Powder
1 ¾ tsps Oregano
3 tbsps Pumpkin Seeds

VEGETABLES

3 tbsps Arugula
3 ¼ cups Asparagus
½ cup Baby Spinach
2 tbsps Basil Leaves
1 cup Cherry Tomatoes
⅓ cup Cilantro
⅓ Cucumber
½ bulb Fennel
2 ⅙ tbsps Fresh Dill
3 Garlic Cloves
2 ⅔ cups Green Beans
1 1/16 head Green Lettuce
1 cup Kale Leaves
⅔ cup Mini Potatoes
1 cup Mixed Greens
1 ½ tsps Parsley
½ cup Portobello
   Mushrooms
½ cup Radishes
2 ¾ Red Bell Peppers
⅓ cup Red Onion
2 leaves Romaine Lettuce
½ Sweet Potato
½ tsp Thyme
1 ¾ cup Tomato
¼ Yellow Bell Pepper
½ Yellow Onion
⅓ Zucchini

PANTRY STAPLES

60 grams Chickpea Pasta
⅔ cup Canned Tomatoes
¾ cup Green Lentils
1 ¾ tbsps Quinoa
¼ can Tuna
4 Brown Rice Cakes
1 tbsp Almond Butter

BAKING

⅓ cup Almond Flour
1 tbsp Monk Fruit
   Sweetener

BREAD, FISH, MEAT & CHEESE

113 grams Chicken Breast
120 grams Chicken Breast
   (cooked)
113 grams Chicken Thighs
   (with skin)
1 Cod Fillet
226 grams Extra Lean
   Ground Beef
113 grams Extra Lean
   Ground Turkey
2 tbsps Feta Cheese
152 grams Halibut Fillet
170 grams Shrimp
100 grams Cooked Turkey
   Breast (sliced)
3 slices Whole Grain Bread
1 Whole Wheat Bun
2 Whole Wheat Tortillas

CONDIMENTS & OILS

1 ½ tbsps. Balsamic Vinegar
1 tsp Coconut Oil
⅔ cup Extra Virgin Olive Oil
2 ⅔ tbsps Pesto
¾ tsp Tamari

FRIDGE

¾ cup Cottage Cheese
10 Eggs
½ cup Plain Coconut Milk
1 ¾ cups Plain Greek Yogurt
1 ¾ tbsps Unsweetened
   Almond Milk

Breakfasts

Quinoa & Kale Egg Muffins

 30 Minutes

 1 Serving

INGREDIENTS

- 1 ½ tsps Extra Virgin Olive Oil
- 1 ¾ tbsps Quinoa (dry)
- 1 tsp Extra Virgin Olive Oil
- 1 cup Kale Leaves (finely chopped)
- ⅓ Tomato (diced)
- 2 Eggs
- 1 ⅓ tbsps Water
- ⅛ tsp Sea Salt

INSTRUCTIONS

1. Preheat oven to 350°F (177°C). Grease a muffin pan with the olive oil or use a silicone muffin tray.
2. Cook the quinoa according to package directions.
3. While cooking the quinoa, heat the oil in a large non-stick pan over medium heat. Add the kale and sauté until wilted and tender, then set aside.
4. Combine the cooked quinoa and the diced tomato to the wilted kale. Divide the quinoa mixture evenly into the muffin tray.
5. Whisk the eggs, water, and salt until well combined. Cover the quinoa, kale, and tomatoes with the egg mix.
6. Bake for about 15 to 18 minutes until the egg is no longer liquid on top.
7. Remove from the oven carefully, allow it to cool, and enjoy!

NUTRITION - AMOUNT PER SERVING

Calories	284	Sugar	1g
Fat	18g	Protein	16g
Carbs	15g	Cholesterol	372mg
Fiber	2g	Sodium	465mg

Almond Pancakes

 20 Minutes

 1 Serving

INGREDIENTS

- ⅓ cup Almond Flour
- ⅓ tsp Baking Powder
- 1 Egg
- 1 ¾ tbsps Unsweetened Almond Milk
- 1 tsp Coconut Oil (softened)
- ⅛ tsp Cinnamon
- ¹⁄₁₆ tsp Sea Salt
- 1 tbsp Almond Butter (for topping)
- 1 tbsp Almonds (roughly sliced, for topping)

INSTRUCTIONS

1. Whisk the almond flour, baking powder, eggs, almond milk, coconut oil, cinnamon, and sea salt in a medium-sized bowl.

2. Heat a greased non-stick skillet over a medium-low heat setting. Spoon ¼ cup of pancake batter into the skillet. Repeat until all the batter is used. Cook each side of the pancake for 3 to 4 minutes until slightly browned.

3. Serve on a plate and top with almond butter and almonds.

NUTRITION - AMOUNT PER SERVING

Calories	480	Sugar	3g
Fat	42g	Protein	20g
Carbs	14g	Cholesterol	186mg
Fiber	7g	Sodium	400mg

Coconut Hemp Seed Breakfast Pudding

 3 Hours

 1 Serving

INGREDIENTS

- ½ cup Plain Coconut Milk (full fat)
- 1 tsp Vanilla Extract
- ¼ cup Hemp Seeds
- 1 ½ tbsps Ground Flax Seeds
- 1 ½ tbsps Chia Seeds
- 1 tsp Unsweetened Shredded Coconut
- ¼ cup Raspberries
- Sweetener (optional, to taste)

INSTRUCTIONS

1. Whisk the coconut milk, vanilla, and optional sweetener in a small mixing bowl. Mix in hemp seeds, ground flax seeds, and chia seeds.
2. Cover the coconut milk and seed mixture. Refrigerate until set, at least 3 hours or overnight.
3. If necessary, thin it with additional coconut milk or water. Serve the pudding with shredded coconut and raspberries on top.

NUTRITION - AMOUNT PER SERVING

Calories	437	Sugar	6g
Fat	32g	Protein	18g
Carbs	22g	Cholesterol	0mg
Fiber	12g	Sodium	24mg

Pesto Eggs & Toast

 15 Minutes

 1 Serving

INGREDIENTS

- 2 tsps Extra Virgin Olive Oil
- 2 Eggs (whisked)
- 2 tsps Pesto
- 2 slices Whole Grain Bread (toasted)
- Sea Salt & Black Pepper (to taste)

INSTRUCTIONS

1. Over medium heat, warm the olive oil in a non-stick pan. Whisk the eggs and pour into the heated pan. Stir with a spatula continuously until they become fluffy and almost set, approximately 2 minutes. Next, gently fold in the pesto until well combined.
2. Serve the eggs on the toast and season with salt and pepper.

NUTRITION - AMOUNT PER SERVING

Calories	485	Sugar	6g
Fat	26g	Protein	25g
Carbs	38g	Cholesterol	372mg
Fiber	6g	Sodium	520mg

Cottage Cheese with Cherries & Pumpkin Seeds

 5 Minutes

 1 Serving

INGREDIENTS

- ¾ cup Cottage Cheese
- 3 tbsps Pumpkin Seeds
- ¼ cup Cherries
- 2 tbsps Walnuts

INSTRUCTIONS

1. Add all the ingredients to a bowl and enjoy!

NUTRITION - AMOUNT PER SERVING

Calories	412	Sugar	10g
Fat	28g	Protein	28g
Carbs	16g	Cholesterol	27mg
Fiber	3g	Sodium	498mg

Plain Omelet & Fruits

 10 Minutes

 1 Serving

INGREDIENTS

- 2 Eggs
- Sea Salt & Black Pepper (to taste)
- 1 tsp Extra Virgin Olive Oil
- ½ cup Mixed Berries

INSTRUCTIONS

1. In a small bowl, whisk the eggs and season with salt and pepper to taste.
2. In a non-stick pan, warm the olive oil over a medium heat setting. Add the eggs and cook until nearly set. Fold the omelet in half, and serve on a plate with fruits on the side.

NUTRITION - AMOUNT PER SERVING

Calories	383	Sugar	16g
Fat	17g	Protein	16g
Carbs	11g	Cholesterol	372mg
Fiber	4g	Sodium	217mg

Eggs & Toast

 5 Minutes

 1 Serving

INGREDIENTS

- 1 tbsp Extra Virgin Olive Oil
- 2 Eggs
- 1 slice Whole Grain Bread (toasted)

INSTRUCTIONS

1. Over a medium heat setting, heat the olive oil in a non-stick pan. Crack the eggs into the pan carefully and cook until done to your liking.
2. Serve the eggs on top of the toast.

NUTRITION - AMOUNT PER SERVING

Calories	372	Sugar	3g
Fat	25g	Protein	18g
Carbs	19g	Cholesterol	372mg
Fiber	3g	Sodium	300mg

Lunches

One Pan Salmon & Fennel with Lime

 35 Minutes

 1 Serving

INGREDIENTS

- ½ bulb Fennel (medium, thinly sliced)
- 1 ½ tbsps Extra Virgin Olive Oil (divided)
- Sea Salt & Black Pepper (to taste)
- 170 grams Salmon Fillet
- 1 Lime (divided)
- ⅛ tsp Fennel Seeds (ground)

INSTRUCTIONS

1. Preheat oven to 400°F (205°C).
2. Add the fennel to a baking dish. Using half of the olive oil, drizzle over the fennel and season with sea salt and black pepper. Toss to combine. Place in the oven and bake for 15 minutes.
3. Pat the salmon dry with paper towel. Once dry, season with sea salt and black pepper. Zest some lime over the top and sprinkle with the fennel seed. Slice half of the lime and set aside.
4. Remove the baking dish with fennel from the oven and place the salmon on top of the fennel. Drizzle with the remaining oil. Scatter the lime slices around. Place back in the oven and bake for 12 to 15 minutes, until cooked through, depending on thickness.
5. Quarter the remaining lime. Serve the fennel and salmon on a plate with the quartered lime, squeezing more lime juice on top if needed.

NUTRITION - AMOUNT PER SERVING

Calories	450	Sugar	5g
Fat	29g	Protein	39g
Carbs	12g	Cholesterol	87mg
Fiber	4g	Sodium	195mg

REFER TO PINEAPPLE ON PAGE 84 FOR QUANTITY AND NUTRITIONAL INFORMATION

One Pan Basil Chicken

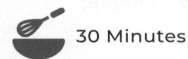 30 Minutes

 1 Serving

INGREDIENTS

- 113 grams Chicken Breast (boneless, skinless, cut into cubes)
- ¼ cup Red Onion (small, thinly sliced)
- 1 cup Green Beans (washed, trimmed)
- 1 ½ tbsps Balsamic Vinegar (divided)
- ⅛ tsp Sea Salt
- ½ (clove, minced)
- 1 tbsp Basil Leaves (fresh, chopped)

INSTRUCTIONS

1. Preheat the oven to 400F (204°C) and line a baking tray with parchment paper. Place the chicken, onion, and green beans on the sheet. Drizzle everything with half the balsamic vinegar and sea salt. Cover the chicken with the minced garlic. Bake for 15 minutes.
2. Take the baking tray out of the oven. Drizzle the remaining balsamic vinegar on top of the chicken and veggies. Add the basil to the chicken and place back in the oven for 5 minutes, or until the chicken is cooked.
3. Remove from the oven and serve.

NUTRITION - AMOUNT PER SERVING

Calories	207	Sugar	9g
Fat	3g	Protein	28g
Carbs	15g	Cholesterol	82mg
Fiber	3g	Sodium	359mg

Lemon Dill Baked Salmon

 25 Minutes

 1 Serving

INGREDIENTS

- 141 grams Salmon Fillet
- 1 tbsp Extra Virgin Olive Oil
- ½ Garlic (cloves, minced)
- 1 ½ tsps Fresh Dill (chopped)
- ¼ Lemon (zested and juiced)
- ¹⁄₁₆ tsp Sea Salt (or more to taste)
- 1 cup Mixed Greens

INSTRUCTIONS

1. Preheat oven to 375°F (191°C).
2. Place the salmon in the middle of a baking tray lined with aluminum foil.
3. Mix the oil, garlic, dill, lemon juice, lemon zest and salt in a small jar. Pour the mix over the salmon. Fold the edges of the foil so that the fish is sealed in a pouch. Bake the pouched salmon for about 16 to 18 minutes or until the salmon flakes with a fork.
4. Take the tray out of the oven. Open the foil and remove the fish. Plate the salmon topped with residual juice from the pouch and serve with mixed greens.

NUTRITION - AMOUNT PER SERVING

Calories	317	Sugar	0g
Fat	20g	Protein	32g
Carbs	2g	Cholesterol	72mg
Fiber	0g	Sodium	276mg

REFER TO PEACH ON PAGE 76 FOR QUANTITY AND NUTRITIONAL INFORMATION

Turkey Pesto Wrap

 5 Minutes

 1 Serving

INGREDIENTS

- 1 tbsp Pesto
- 1 Whole Wheat Tortilla (large)
- 100 grams Cooked Turkey Breast (sliced or chopped)
- ¹⁄₁₆ head Green Lettuce (leaves separated)
- ½ Tomato (large, sliced)
- ¼ tsp Sea Salt

INSTRUCTIONS

1. Spread the pesto onto the tortilla.
2. Arrange the turkey, lettuce, and tomato on top. Season the tomatoes with salt. Roll tightly into a wrap, tucking in the sides, and enjoy!

NUTRITION - AMOUNT PER SERVING

Calories	307	Sugar	3g
Fat	14g	Protein	21g
Carbs	24g	Cholesterol	49mg
Fiber	5g	Sodium	1853mg

Chicken Avocado Wrap

 10 Minutes

 1 Serving

INGREDIENTS

- 50 grams Avocado (mashed, diced)
- 1 ½ tsps Lime Juice
- 1 Whole Wheat Tortilla
- Sea Salt & Black Pepper (to taste)
- 2 leaves Romaine (medium, chopped)
- ¼ cup Cherry Tomatoes (halved or quartered)
- 120 grams Cooked Chicken Breast (sliced or chopped)

INSTRUCTIONS

1. In a small bowl, mash 30 grams of the avocado with the lime juice. Spread the mashed avocado in the center of the tortilla. Season with salt and pepper to taste.
2. Dice the remaining avocado.
3. Place the lettuce, tomatoes, diced avocado, and sliced chicken on top of the mashed avocado and roll the tortilla around the filling.

NUTRITION - AMOUNT PER SERVING

Calories	406	Sugar	3g
Fat	15g	Protein	43g
Carbs	27g	Cholesterol	125mg
Fiber	9g	Sodium	325mg

REFER TO PINEAPPLE ON PAGE 84 FOR QUANTITY AND NUTRITIONAL INFORMATION

Lemon Cilantro Cod with Peppers

 35 Minutes

 1 Serving

INGREDIENTS

- 1 ½ tbsps Lemon Juice
- 1 ½ tbsps Extra Virgin Olive Oil (divided)
- ⅓ cup Cilantro (finely chopped, divided)
- ¼ tsp Sea Salt (divided)
- 1 Cod Fillet
- ¼ Red Bell Pepper (sliced)
- ¼ Yellow Bell Pepper (sliced)
- ½ Tomato (diced)

INSTRUCTIONS

1. Preheat oven to 375°F (190°C).
2. Combine the lemon juice, ⅔ oil, ⅔ cilantro, and ½ sea salt in a zipper-lock bag. Add the cod and gently massage the marinade into the fillet. Marinate for at least 15 minutes.
3. Meanwhile, warm the remaining oil over a medium heat setting. Add the bell peppers and diced tomato, and sauté for 8 to 10 minutes until the peppers are soft and the tomato juices have been released. Add the remaining cilantro and salt and stir. Remove from heat.
4. Place the cod in a baking dish. Cover the dish with a lid or use aluminum foil. Bake for 18 to 20 minutes until the fish is cooked and flakes easily.
5. Remove from heat after cooking for about 15 minutes. Place the cooked peppers on top of the cod fillets and cook for the remaining time uncovered.
6. Serve the fish and peppers on a plate and season with additional salt if needed.

NUTRITION - AMOUNT PER SERVING

Calories	404	Sugar	2g
Fat	22g	Protein	43g
Carbs	8g	Cholesterol	99mg
Fiber	2g	Sodium	743mg

REFER TO BANANA ON PAGE 78 FOR QUANTITY AND NUTRITIONAL INFORMATION

One Pan Halibut & Green Beans

 **20 Minutes**

 **1 Serving**

INGREDIENTS

- ⅓ Lemon (zested and juiced)
- 2 tsps Extra Virgin Olive Oil
- 1 tsp Fresh Dill (stems removed, chopped)
- ¹⁄₁₆ tsp Sea Salt
- 1⅔ cups Green Beans (trimmed)
- 152 grams Halibut Fillet

INSTRUCTIONS

1. Preheat oven to 400°F (205°C). Line a baking tray with parchment paper.
2. Whisk the lemon zest and juice, oil, dill, and salt together in a large bowl.
3. Add the green beans to the marinade and gently toss until well-coated. Transfer to the baking tray.
4. Add the halibut to the marinade and coat evenly. Transfer to the baking tray alongside the green beans.
5. Cook for 10 to 12 minutes until the halibut flakes easily and the green beans are tender. Plate the halibut on top of the beans to enjoy!

NUTRITION - AMOUNT PER SERVING

Calories	272	Sugar	6g
Fat	11g	Protein	31g
Carbs	13g	Cholesterol	74mg
Fiber	5g	Sodium	212mg

REFER TO PEACH ON PAGE 76 FOR QUANTITY AND NUTRITIONAL INFORMATION

Dinners

Zucchini & Ground Beef Skillet

 25 Minutes

 1 Serving

INGREDIENTS

- 113 grams Extra Lean Ground Beef
- ½ Garlic (cloves, minced)
- Sea Salt & Black Pepper (to taste)
- ⅔ cup Diced Tomatoes (canned with juices)
- ⅓ Zucchini (medium, chopped)
- ⅓ tsp Cumin
- ¹⁄₁₆ tsp Onion Powder

INSTRUCTIONS

1. Over a medium heat setting warm a non-stick pan. Add the ground beef, garlic, salt, and pepper and cook for approximately 10 minutes, breaking it up as it cooks. Drain extra fat if needed.
2. Add the diced tomatoes, cumin, and onion powder. Mix, cover, and let simmer for 10 minutes. Mix in the zucchini and cook covered for a further 5 minutes. Serve on a plate and enjoy!

NUTRITION - AMOUNT PER SERVING

Calories	246	Sugar	5g
Fat	12g	Protein	25g
Carbs	8g	Cholesterol	74mg
Fiber	2g	Sodium	106mg

REFER TO APPLE ON PAGE 44 FOR QUANTITY AND NUTRITIONAL INFORMATION

Shrimp Asparagus Pesto Pasta

 **30 Minutes**

 **1 Serving**

INGREDIENTS

- 1 ½ cups Asparagus (chopped into 1-inch pieces)
- 170 grams Shrimp (uncooked, shells on)
- 1 tbsp Extra Virgin Olive Oil
- ¹⁄₁₆ tsp Sea Salt (or more to taste)
- ½ Lemon (sliced into rounds)
- 60 grams Chickpea Pasta
- 1 tbsp Pesto

INSTRUCTIONS

1. Preheat oven to 400°F (204°C).
2. Lay the asparagus and shrimp on a baking sheet. Drizzle with olive oil ensuring everything is coated. Sprinkle with sea salt and top with lemon slices. Bake for 15 to 18 minutes until the shrimp are cooked and have turned pink. Remove from the oven and set aside for later.
3. While the shrimp and asparagus bake, boil a medium saucepan with water. Add the chickpea pasta to the boiling water. Follow the instruction on the pasta packaging to cook the pasta. . Once cooked, rinse and drain the pasta, then return it to the pot. Stir in the pesto and mix well to combine.
4. Remove shells from shrimp. Mix the shrimp and asparagus into the pasta and serve in a bowl.

NUTRITION - AMOUNT PER SERVING

Calories	564	Sugar	10g
Fat	24g	Protein	54g
Carbs	43g	Cholesterol	274mg
Fiber	13g	Sodium	509mg

REFER TO GRAPES ON PAGE 36 FOR QUANTITY AND NUTRITIONAL INFORMATION

Nicoise Salad

 30 Minutes

 1 Serving

INGREDIENTS

- ⅔ cup Mini Potatoes (halved)
- ¾ cup Asparagus (trimmed)
- 1 ½ tsps Lemon Juice
- 2 ¼ tsps Extra Virgin Olive Oil
- ¾ tsp Fresh Dill (chopped, plus extra for optional garnish)
- Sea Salt & Black Pepper (to taste)
- ¼ can Tuna (drained)
- ⅓ cup Cherry Tomatoes (halved)
- ¼ cup Radishes (quartered or sliced)
- ¼ Avocado (sliced)
- 1⁄16 Cucumber (medium, sliced)
- 1 ⅓ tbsps Red Onion (sliced)

INSTRUCTIONS

1. Add the mini potatoes to a medium sized post and cover them with cold water. Bring the water to a boil and cook for 10 minutes or until tender. Drain the potatoes as soon as they are cooked and transfer them immediately to an ice bath to cool.

2. Place the asparagus in a steaming basket over boiling water and cover. Steam for about 3 to 5 minutes or until tender. Transfer the steamed asparagus to an ice bath to cool.

3. Combine the lemon juice, oil, and dill in a small bowl. Season with salt and pepper.

4. Arrange the tuna, cherry tomatoes, radishes, avocado, cucumber, cooked potatoes, and asparagus on a serving platter. Top with red onion and garnish with extra dill if required. Spoon the dressing on top to enjoy!

NUTRITION - AMOUNT PER SERVING

Calories	323	Sugar	6g
Fat	18g	Protein	14g
Carbs	30g	Cholesterol	15mg
Fiber	9g	Sodium	129mg

REFER TO CHERRIES ON PAGE 78 FOR QUANTITY AND NUTRIONAL INFORMATION

Turkey Burger

 20 Minutes

 1 Serving

INGREDIENTS

- 113 grams Extra Lean Ground Turkey
- ½ Tomato (chopped)
- ½ Tomato (sliced)
- ½ tsp Oregano (dried)
- 1 ½ tsps Parsley (chopped)
- ¼ Egg
- ¹⁄₁₆ tsp Sea Salt
- 2 ¼ tsps Extra Virgin Olive Oil
- 3 tbsps Arugula
- 1 Whole Wheat Bun

INSTRUCTIONS

1. Combine the turkey, chopped tomatoes, oregano, parsley, egg, and salt in a large bowl. Once mixed, form into a patty and set aside.
2. Add oil to a heated cast-iron skillet over medium heat and add the oil. Add the burger patty and cook for five minutes per side or until cooked through.
3. Place the arugula on the bottom of the burger bun and top with the turkey burger patty and sliced tomato. Add the top half of the bun to form a delicious burger.

NUTRITION - AMOUNT PER SERVING

Calories	428	Sugar	3g
Fat	23g	Protein	30g
Carbs	28g	Cholesterol	130mg
Fiber	4g	Sodium	526mg

REFER TO GRAPES ON PAGE 36 FOR QUANTITY AND NUTRITIONAL INFORMATION

One Pan Chicken Thighs with Asparagus

 35 Minutes

 1 Serving

INGREDIENTS

- 113 grams Chicken Thighs with Skin
- ½ tsp Oregano (dried)
- ½ tsp Thyme (dried)
- ⅛ tsp Sea Salt (divided)
- 1 ½ tsps Extra Virgin Olive Oil (divided)
- ½ Sweet Potato (large, chopped)
- 1 cup Asparagus (trimmed)

INSTRUCTIONS

1. Preheat oven to 425°F (218°C). Line a baking tray with parchment paper.
2. Season the chicken thighs with oregano, thyme and half of the sea salt. Drizzle half of the oil on top of the sweet potato and place next to the chicken. Bake for 20 minutes.
3. Remove the baking tray and add the asparagus along with the remaining oil and sea salt. Bake for a further 15 minutes until the chicken is cooked, the sweet potatoes have browned and the asparagus is tender.

NUTRITION - AMOUNT PER SERVING

Calories	394	Sugar	5g
Fat	26g	Protein	23g
Carbs	19g	Cholesterol	111mg
Fiber	5g	Sodium	425mg

Lentil Stuffed Grilled Peppers

 30 Minutes

 1 Serving

INGREDIENTS

- ⅓ tsp Extra Virgin Olive Oil
- ¼ Yellow Onion (diced)
- ½ cup Portobello Mushroom (chopped)
- ¼ cup Cherry Tomatoes (halved)
- ¾ tsp Tamari
- ½ Garlic (cloves, minced)
- 1/16 tsp Sea Salt
- 1/16 tsp Black Pepper
- 1/16 tsp Cayenne Pepper (optional)
- 1 tbsp Basil Leaves (chopped)
- ½ cup Baby Spinach (chopped)
- 2 Red Bell Pepper
- 2 tbsps Feta Cheese (crumbled)
- ¾ cup Green Lentils (cooked, drained and rinsed)

INSTRUCTIONS

1. Heat oven to 425°F (218°C).
2. Heat olive oil in a skillet over medium heat. Add onion, mushrooms, cherry tomatoes, and tamari. Sauté for 5 minutes until the onion is translucent. Mix in minced garlic, sea salt, black pepper, and cayenne, and sauté for 1 minute. Add the basil and spinach and, stirring occasionally, cook until just wilted. Remove the vegetable mix from the heat and set aside to cool while you prepare the red peppers.
3. Cut off the stem, chop the top of the peppers off, and carve out the seeds.
4. Add the lentils and feta cheese to the skillet with the vegetables and stir well to distribute them evenly. Use a spoon to pack this vegetable mix into the red peppers. Place the peppers on a baking sheet.
5. Heat the oven to 425°F (218°C). Bake the stuffed peppers in the oven for 20 minutes. Remove, drizzle with a little olive oil and serve.

NUTRITION - AMOUNT PER SERVING

Calories	342	Sugar	17g
Fat	7g	Protein	22g
Carbs	53g	Cholesterol	17mg
Fiber	20g	Sodium	647mg

REFER TO CHERRIES ON PAGE 78 FOR QUANTITY AND NUTRITIONAL INFORMATION

Beef Burrito Bowl with Cauliflower Rice

 30 Minutes

 1 Serving

INGREDIENTS

- 1 ½ tsps Extra Virgin Olive Oil (divided)
- 1 Garlic (cloves, minced)
- ¼ Yellow Onion (small, finely diced)
- 113 grams Extra Lean Ground Beef
- ¾ tsp Cumin (ground)
- ¾ tsp Coriander (ground)
- ¾ tsp Oregano (dried)
- ⅓ tsp Sea Salt (divided)
- ¼ Lime (juiced)
- 1 cup Cauliflower Rice
- ½ Avocado (diced)

INSTRUCTIONS

1. Over a medium heating setting, heat half of the olive oil in a non-stick skillet. Add garlic and onions and sauté for 2 minutes until onions become translucent.
2. Add ground beef to the skillet. Break up the beef as it cooks, until no longer pink.
3. When the ground beef is cooked, drain any excess oil. Put back over medium heat and add the cumin, coriander, oregano, half of the salt, and lime juice to the skillet. Stir to coat the beef with the spice and cook for another minute until very fragrant. Transfer to a dish and cover to keep warm.
4. Place the skillet back over the heat and add the remaining olive oil. Add the cauliflower rice and season with remaining sea salt. Cook the cauliflower rice, stirring occasionally, until cauliflower is warmed through and just tender.
5. Serve the cauliflower rice in a bowl topped with the seasoned beef and diced avocado.

NUTRITION - AMOUNT PER SERVING

Calories	481	Sugar	5g
Fat	33g	Protein	28g
Carbs	19g	Cholesterol	74mg
Fiber	11g	Sodium	997mg

REFER TO APPLE ON PAGE 44 FOR QUANTITY AND NUTRITIONAL INFORMATION

Snacks

Cherries & Greek Yogurt

 5 Minutes

 1 Serving

INGREDIENTS

- ½ cup Plain Greek Yogurt
- ½ cup Cherries (pitted)

INSTRUCTIONS

1. Serve the yogurt with the cherries.

NUTRITION - AMOUNT PER SERVING

Calories	139	Sugar	13g
Fat	3g	Protein	12g
Carbs	18g	Cholesterol	17mg
Fiber	2g	Sodium	70mg

Avocado Rice Cakes

 5 Minutes

 1 Serving

INGREDIENTS

- ½ Avocado
- ½ tsps Lime Juice
- Sea Salt & Black Pepper (to taste)
- 2 Brown Rice Cakes
- Red Pepper Flakes (optional)

INSTRUCTIONS

1. Mash the avocado, lime juice, sea salt, and black pepper with a fork and spread over the rice cakes. For extra flavor, sprinkle with red pepper flakes (optional).

NUTRITION - AMOUNT PER SERVING

Calories	281	Sugar	1g
Fat	16g	Protein	4g
Carbs	37g	Cholesterol	0mg
Fiber	9g	Sodium	7mg

Creamy Mango Pudding

 5 Minutes

 1 Serving

INGREDIENTS

- ½ cup Frozen Mango
- ½ cup Plain Greek Yogurt

INSTRUCTIONS

1. Use a blender to thoroughly blend the mango and yogurt until smooth and well combined. Transfer to a glass and enjoy!

NUTRITION - AMOUNT PER SERVING

Calories	140	Sugar	14g
Fat	3g	Protein	12g
Carbs	18g	Cholesterol	17mg
Fiber	1g	Sodium	71mg

Lemon Dill Yogurt Dip & Peppers

 5 Minutes

 1 Serving

INGREDIENTS

- ½ cup Plain Greek Yogurt
- ¼ Lemon (juiced)
- 1 tbsp Fresh Dill (finely chopped)
- ½ Red Bell Pepper (large, sliced)

INSTRUCTIONS

1. Mix together the yogurt, lemon juice, and dill in a bowl. Serve alongside the sliced bell peppers.

NUTRITION - AMOUNT PER SERVING

Calories	109	Sugar	6g
Fat	3g	Protein	12g
Carbs	10g	Cholesterol	17mg
Fiber	1g	Sodium	73mg

Strawberries & Almonds

 5 Minutes

 1 Serving

INGREDIENTS

- 1 cup Strawberries
- ¼ cup Almonds

INSTRUCTIONS

1. Add the strawberries and almonds to a bowl to enjoy!

NUTRITION - AMOUNT PER SERVING

Calories	253	Sugar	9g
Fat	18g	Protein	9g
Carbs	19g	Cholesterol	0mg
Fiber	7g	Sodium	2mg

Radish & Cucumber Rice Cakes

 10 Minutes

 1 Serving

INGREDIENTS

- 2 Brown Rice Cakes
- ¼ cup Radishes (sliced)
- ¼ Cucumber (sliced)
- Sea Salt & Black Pepper (to taste)

INSTRUCTIONS

1. Top each rice cake with the radishes and cucumber. Sprinkle with salt and pepper.

NUTRITION - AMOUNT PER SERVING

Calories	136	Sugar	2g
Fat	1g	Protein	3g
Carbs	32g	Cholesterol	0mg
Fiber	3g	Sodium	13mg

Greek Yogurt with Almonds & Pear

 5 Minutes

 1 Serving

INGREDIENTS

- ¼ cup Plain Greek Yogurt
- 2 tbsps Almonds
- 1 Pear (sliced)

INSTRUCTIONS

1. Add all ingredients to a bowl.

NUTRITION - AMOUNT PER SERVING

Calories	250	Sugar	20g
Fat	10g	Protein	10g
Carbs	34g	Cholesterol	8mg
Fiber	8g	Sodium	37mg

BONUS RECIPES

Desserts

Apple Wedges with Peanut Butter & Chocolate

 20 Minutes

 1 Serving

INGREDIENTS

- 2 tbsps Dark Chocolate Chips
- ¼ tsp Coconut Oil
- ½ Apple (cut into wedges)
- 2 ¼ tsps All Natural Peanut Butter

INSTRUCTIONS

1. Place chocolate chips and coconut oil in a small microwaveable bowl and microwave on high for 30 to 45-second intervals until melted. Stir with a spoon to fully combine after each interval.
2. Place the apple slices on a plate. Drizzle with the melted chocolate and transfer to the fridge to let the chocolate harden, about 10 to 15 minutes. Spoon the peanut butter onto the plate and enjoy!

NUTRITION - AMOUNT PER SERVING

Calories	310	Sugar	25g
Fat	17g	Protein	5g
Carbs	31g	Cholesterol	0mg
Fiber	3g	Sodium	3mg

Coconut Mug Cake

 5 Minutes

 1 Serving

INGREDIENTS

- 1 ½ tsps Coconut Oil (melted)
- 3 cups Plain Coconut Milk (full fat)
- 1 tbsp Monk Fruit Sweetener
- 1 ½ tbsps Almond Flour
- 1 tbsp Coconut Flour
- 1 tbsp Unsweetened Shredded Coconut
- ¼ tsp Baking Powder

INSTRUCTIONS

1. Mix melted coconut oil and coconut milk in a mug, add in the monk fruit sweetener, and stir well. Form a thick batter by stirring in almond flour, coconut flour, coconut, and baking powder.
2. Microwave for approximately 90 seconds until the cake is spongy and cooked. Let the cake cool before removing it from the mug. Plate and top with extra shredded coconut if required.

NUTRITION - AMOUNT PER SERVING

Calories	422	Sugar	22g
Fat	31g	Protein	4g
Carbs	41g	Cholesterol	0mg
Fiber	4g	Sodium	247mg

Super Seed Chocolate Bark

 40 Minutes

 1 Serving

INGREDIENTS

- 20 grams Dark Chocolate
- ½ tsp Coconut Oil
- 1 tbsp Pumpkin Seeds
- 1 tbsp Sunflower Seeds
- 1 ½ tsps Hemp Seeds

INSTRUCTIONS

1. Line a baking tray with parchment paper.
2. Fill a medium-sized pot with an inch of water. Place a heat-safe bowl on top of the pot which should rest tightly on top of the pot so no water or steam escapes. The bowl should not touch the water in the pot below.
3. Bring the water to a boil, then reduce heat to a low setting.
4. Add the coconut oil and dark chocolate to the bowl and stir until the chocolate has completely melted.
5. Remove the bowl and stir in all the seeds until the seeds are completely covered in chocolate.
6. Pour the chocolate bark mixture onto the parchment paper spreading to form an even layer. Place the chocolate bark in the freezer for about half an hour until solid.
7. Remove the chocolate from the freezer and break it into pieces. Store the chocolate bark in the fridge until ready to eat.

NUTRITION - AMOUNT PER SERVING

Calories	252	Sugar	5g
Fat	21g	Protein	7g
Carbs	12g	Cholesterol	1mg
Fiber	4g	Sodium	5mg

Peanut Butter Mocha Chia Pudding

 3 Hours 10 Minutes

 1 Serving

INGREDIENTS

- ½ cup Canned Coconut Milk
- 2 tbsps Coffee (brewed drip or espresso)
- 1 ½ tsps Cacao Powder
- 1 ⅓ tbsps Chia Seeds
- 1 ½ tsps All Natural Peanut Butter
- ¹⁄₁₆ tsp Stevia Powder (to taste)

INSTRUCTIONS

1. Blend all the ingredients in a blender until completely smooth, for at least 1 minute, Scoop into a glass or jar and refrigerate overnight or for at least 3 hours.

NUTRITION - AMOUNT PER SERVING

Calories	353	Sugar	2g
Fat	31g	Protein	6g
Carbs	13g	Cholesterol	0mg
Fiber	7g	Sodium	35mg

Dark Chocolate, Blueberry & Walnut Cups

 40 Minutes

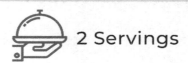 2 Servings

INGREDIENTS

- ¾ tsp Coconut Oil
- 60 grams Dark Chocolate (coarsely chopped)
- ¾ tsp Chia Seeds
- 2 tbsps Blueberries
- 2 tsps Walnuts (finely chopped)

INSTRUCTIONS

1. Place muffin liners in a muffin tray or use a silicone muffin tray.
2. Melt the coconut oil and chopped chocolate in a saucepan over low heat, stirring constantly. Remove from the heat and stir in the chia seeds.
3. Distribute the chocolate mixture evenly among the muffin cups. Top each with equal amounts of blueberries and walnuts, gently pressing them into the chocolate.
4. Chill in the fridge for at least 30 minutes.

NUTRITION - AMOUNT PER SERVING

Calories	219	Sugar	8g
Fat	16g	Protein	3g
Carbs	16g	Cholesterol	1mg
Fiber	4g	Sodium	6mg

Smoothies

Blueberry Energy Smoothie

 10 Minutes

 1 Serving

INGREDIENTS

- ¼ cup Cashews
- 2 tbsps Hemp Seeds
- 1 cup Baby Spinach
- ¾ cup Frozen Blueberries
- 1 cup Unsweetened Almond Milk

INSTRUCTIONS

1. Combine cashews, hemp seeds, and milk in a blender. Blend until very smooth.
2. Add in baby spinach and frozen blueberries. Blend again until smooth. Pour into a glass and enjoy!

NUTRITION - AMOUNT PER SERVING

Calories	403	Sugar	12g
Fat	29g	Protein	14g
Carbs	29g	Cholesterol	0mg
Fiber	18g	Sodium	192mg

Winter Berry Smoothie

 10 Minutes

 1 Serving

INGREDIENTS

- ¾ cup unsweetened Almond Milk
- 1 ½ tsps Ground Flax Seed
- 1 ½ tsps Hemp Seeds
- ½ Navel Orange (peeled and sectioned)
- ¾ cup Frozen Berries
- 1 cup Baby Spinach

INSTRUCTIONS

1. Combine all the ingredients in a blender until completely smooth. Pour into a glass and enjoy!

NUTRITION - AMOUNT PER SERVING

Calories	168	Sugar	17g
Fat	6g	Protein	6g
Carbs	27g	Cholesterol	0mg
Fiber	8g	Sodium	145mg

Detox Green Smoothie

 10 Minutes

 1 Serving

INGREDIENTS

- 2 cups Kale Leaves
- ½ Cucumber (chopped)
- ½ Lemon (juiced)
- 1 Pear (peeled and chopped)
- 1 ½ tsps Ginger (grated)
- 1 ½ tsps Ground Flax Seed
- ¾ cup Water
- 2 ½ Ice Cubes

INSTRUCTIONS

1. Combine all ingredients together in a blender until completely mixed and smooth.
2. Pour into a glass and enjoy!

NUTRITION - AMOUNT PER SERVING

Calories	164	Sugar	21g
Fat	2g	Protein	4g
Carbs	38g	Cholesterol	0mg
Fiber	9g	Sodium	31mg

Citrus Avocado Smoothie

 10 Minutes

 1 Serving

INGREDIENTS

- ½ Avocado
- ⅓ Cucumber (medium)
- 1 Lime (juiced, zested)
- 4 Ice Cubes
- Sea Salt & Black Pepper (to taste, optional)

INSTRUCTIONS

1. Combine all the ingredients in a blender until mixed and completely smooth.
2. Pour into a glass and enjoy!

NUTRITION - AMOUNT PER SERVING

Calories	187	Sugar	3g
Fat	15g	Protein	3g
Carbs	16g	Cholesterol	0mg
Fiber	7g	Sodium	10mg

Berry Coconut Smoothie

 5 Minutes

 1 Serving

INGREDIENTS

- 1 cup Plain Coconut Milk (full fat)
- ½ cup Frozen Berries
- ¼ Avocado

INSTRUCTIONS

1. Pour all of the ingredients into a blender and blend until smooth.
2. Pour into a glass and enjoy!

NUTRITION - AMOUNT PER SERVING

Calories	200	Sugar	15g
Fat	12g	Protein	2g
Carbs	21g	Cholesterol	0mg
Fiber	6g	Sodium	40mg

Snacks

Savory Chickpea Muffins

 45 Minutes

 1 Serving

INGREDIENTS

- ½ cup Chickpea Flour
- ¼ tsp Baking Powder
- ¼ tsp Garlic Powder
- ¼ tsp Sea Salt
- 1 tbsp Extra Virgin Olive Oil
- ¼ cup Water
- ¼ cup Mushrooms (chopped)
- ¼ cup Arugula (chopped, tightly packed)

INSTRUCTIONS

1. Preheat oven to 350°F (175°C). Use a silicone muffin tray or line a muffin tray.
2. Combine chickpea flour, baking powder, garlic powder, and salt in a large mixing bowl. Mix well. Add the oil and water. Mix with a fork until a thick, pancake-like batter forms.
3. Stir in the mushrooms and arugula until well combined. Spoon ⅓ cup into each muffin cup. Transfer to the oven and bake for 35 minutes until starting to brown.
4. Plate and enjoy!

NUTRITION - AMOUNT PER SERVING

Calories	307	Sugar	6g
Fat	17g	Protein	11g
Carbs	28g	Cholesterol	0mg
Fiber	5g	Sodium	746mg

Cucumber Tuna Bites

 5 Minutes

 1 Serving

INGREDIENTS

- 1 can Tuna (flaked and drained)
- 2 tbsps Cream Cheese, Regular
- 1 Cucumber (large, sliced into rounds)

INSTRUCTIONS

1. Add the tuna to a small bowl with the cream cheese and combine well.
2. To serve, add a spoonful of the tuna mixture on top of each cucumber round.

NUTRITION - AMOUNT PER SERVING

Calories	276	Sugar	6g
Fat	10g	Protein	36g
Carbs	12g	Cholesterol	86mg
Fiber	2g	Sodium	544mg

Sweet Potato & Coconut Bites

 40 Minutes

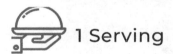 1 Serving

INGREDIENTS

- 1 Sweet Potato (large, cut into cubes)
- 1 tbsp Extra Virgin Olive Oil
- ⅓ cup Unsweetened Shredded Coconut
- 2 ¼ tsps Cinnamon

INSTRUCTIONS

1. Preheat oven to 350°F (177°C). Line a baking tray with parchment paper.
2. Add the sweet potatoes, oil, shredded coconut and cinnamon into a bowl. Toss together until combined.
3. Transfer the potatoes to the baking tray and place in the oven for 30 to 35 minutes, flipping them at the halfway point to ensure they are brown and crispy on both sides.
4. Remove from the oven and plate.

NUTRITION - AMOUNT PER SERVING

Calories	423	Sugar	38g
Fat	7g	Protein	0mg
Carbs	31g	Cholesterol	11g
Fiber	4g	Sodium	81mg

Kale & Zucchini Mini Egg White Bites

 25 Minutes

 1 Serving

INGREDIENTS

- ¾ cup Egg Whites
- ¾ cup Kale Leaves (finely chopped)
- ⅓ Zucchini (medium, finely diced)
- ⅛ tsp Garlic Powder
- ⅛ tsp Onion Powder
- ⅛ tsp Sea Salt

INSTRUCTIONS

1. Preheat oven to 350°F (175°C).
2. Mix the egg whites, kale, zucchini, garlic powder, onion powder, and salt in a bowl.
3. Scoop the mixture into lined muffin cups. Bake for 20 minutes or until cooked through.
4. Let cool before serving.

NUTRITION - AMOUNT PER SERVING

Calories	114	Sugar	3g
Fat	1g	Protein	21g
Carbs	5g	Cholesterol	0mg
Fiber	1g	Sodium	612mg

Pomegranate Yogurt Bites

 2 Hours 10 Minutes

 1 Serving

INGREDIENTS

- 1 cup Unsweetened Coconut Yogurt
- ¼ tsp Vanilla Extract
- ¾ cup Pomegranate Seeds

INSTRUCTIONS

1. Line a baking sheet with parchment paper.
2. In a bowl, mix the yogurt, vanilla, and pomegranate seeds.
3. Spoon the yogurt onto the parchment paper in clusters. Transfer to the freezer until set, about 2 hours.
4. When ready to enjoy, let them sit for 5 to 8 minutes to soften.

NUTRITION - AMOUNT PER SERVING

Calories	204	Sugar	15g
Fat	8g	Protein	2g
Carbs	32g	Cholesterol	0mg
Fiber	7g	Sodium	50mg

Food Translations

Depending on where you are in the world, some foods are known by different names. If you see an ingredient that you are not familiar with, check the chart below to see if it has a name you will recognize.

USA	UK	AUSTRALIA
ALL PURPOSE FLOUR	PLAIN FLOUR	PLAIN FLOUR
ARUGULA	ROCKET	ROCKET
BUTTERNUT SQUASH	BUTTERNUT SQUASH	BUTTERNUT PUMPKIN
BELL PEPPERS	PEPPERS	CAPSICUM
CREMINI MUSHROOMS	CHESTNUT MUSHROOMS	PORTOBELLO MUSHROOMS
CILANTRO	CORIANDER	CORIANDER / CILANTRO
COLLARD GREENS	GREENS	GREENS
CORNSTARCH	CORNFLOUR	CORNFLOUR
EGGPLANT	AUBERGINE	EGGPLANT
SNOW PEAS	MANGETOUT	SNOW PEAS
GARBANZO BEANS	CHICKPEAS	CHICKPEAS
GROUND BEEF	MINCED BEEF	MINCE
PAPAYA	PAW PAW	PAW PAW
WHITE NAVY BEANS	CANNELLINI BEANS	CANNELLINI BEANS
POWDERED SUGAR	ICING SUGAR	ICING SUGAR
ROMAINE LETTUCE	COS LETTUCE	COS LETTUCE
BOSTON LETTUCE	BUTTER LETTUCE	GREEN BUTTER LETTUCE
GREEN ONIONS	SPRING ONIONS	SCALLIONS
SHRIMP	PRAWN	PRAWN
SWISS CHARD	CHARD	SILVERBEET
ZUCCHINI	COURGETTE	ZUCCHINI

Cooking Conversions

CUP	ONCES	MILLILITERS	TBSP
8 cup	64 oz	1895 ml	128
6 cup	48 oz	1420 ml	96
5 cup	40 oz	1180 ml	80
4 cup	32 oz	960 ml	64
2 cup	16 oz	500 ml	32
1 cup	8 oz	250 ml	16
3/4 cup	6 oz	177 ml	12
2/3 cup	5 oz	158 ml	11
1/2 cup	4 oz	118 ml	8
3/8 cup	3 oz	90 ml	6
1/3 cup	2.5 oz	79 ml	5.5
1/4 cup	2 oz	59 ml	4
1/8 cup	1 oz	30 ml	3
1/16 cup	1/2 oz	15 ml	1

IMPERIAL	METRIC
1/2 oz	15 g
1 oz	29 g
2 oz	57 g
3 oz	85 g
4 oz	113 g
5 oz	141 g
6 oz	170 g
8 oz	227 g
10 oz	283 g
12 oz	340 g
13 oz	369 g
14 oz	397 g
15 oz	425 g
1 lb	453 g

FAHRENHEIT	CELSIUS
100 °F	37 °C
150 °F	65 °C
200 °F	93 °C
250 °F	121 °C
300 °F	150 °C
325 °F	160 °C
350 °F	180 °C

FAHRENHEIT	CELSIUS
350 °F	180 °C
375 °F	190 °C
400 °F	200 °C
425 °F	220 °C
450 °F	230 °C
500 °F	260 °C
525 °F	274 °C
550 °F	288 °C